AUSTRALIANA FACSIMILE EDITIONS No. 4

Public Library of South Australia

Adelaide

1963

TWO EXPEDITIONS

INTO THE INTERIOR OF

SOUTHERN AUSTRALIA.

VOL. I.

TWO EXPEDITIONS

INTO THE INTERIOR OF

SOUTHERN AUSTRALIA,

DURING THE YEARS

1828, 1829, 1830, and 1831:

WITH OBSERVATIONS

ON

THE SOIL, CLIMATE, AND GENERAL RESOURCES

OF THE COLONY OF

𝔑𝔢𝔴 𝔖𝔬𝔲𝔱𝔥 𝔚𝔞𝔩𝔢𝔰.

BY CAPT. CHARLES STURT, 39TH REGT.
F.L.S. AND F.R.G.S.

" For though most men are contented only to see a river as it runs by them, and talk of the changes in it as they happen; when it is troubled, or when clear; when it drowns the country in a flood, or forsakes it in a drought : yet he that would know the nature of the water, and the causes of those accidents (so as to guess at their continuance or return), must find out its source, and observe with what strength it rises, what length it runs, and how many small streams fall in, and feed it to such a height, as make it either delightful or terrible to the eye, and useful or danger-ous to the country about it."—*Sir William Temple's Netherlands.*

IN TWO VOLUMES.

VOL. I.

LONDON:

SMITH, ELDER AND CO., 65, CORNHILL.

1833.

LONDON :
PRINTED BY STEWART AND CO.
OLD BAILEY.

THE EARL OF RIPON,

VISCOUNT GODERICH,

Lord Privy Seal,

&c. &c. &c.

My Lord,.

THE completion of this Work affords me
the opportunity I have long desired of thanking
your Lordship thus publicly, for the kindness
with which you acceded to my request to be
permitted to dedicate it to you.

The encouragement your Lordship was pleased
to give me has served to stimulate me in the prosecution of a task, which would, I fear, have been
too great for me to have accomplished, in my
present condition, under any ordinary views of
ambition. Indeed, labouring as I have been for

A

many months past, under an almost total depriva-
tion of sight, (the effect of exposure and anxiety
of mind in the prosecution of geographical researches,) I owe it to the casual assistance of some
of my friends, that I am at length enabled to lay
these results before your Lordship and the public.

While I feel a painful conviction that many
errors must necessarily pervade a work produced
under such unfavourable circumstances, it affords
me no small consolation to reflect that your Lordship has been aware of my situation, and will be
disposed to grant me every reasonable indulgence.

I have the honor to be,

With the highest respect,

My Lord,

Your Lordship's

Very obedient and humble Servant,

CHARLES STURT.

London,
June, 1833.

PRELIMINARY CHAPTER.

WHEN I first determined on committing to the press a detailed account of the two expeditions, which I conducted into the interior of the Australian continent, pursuant to the orders of Lieutenant General Darling, the late Governor of the Colony of New South Wales, it was simply

with a view of laying their results before the
geographical world, and of correcting the opinions that prevailed with regard to the unexplored country to the westward of the Blue
Mountains. I did not feel myself equal either
to the task or the responsibility of venturing
any remarks on the Colony of New South Wales
itself. I had had little time for inquiry, amidst
the various duties that fell to my lot in the ordinary routine of the service to which I belonged,
when unemployed by the Colonial Government
in the prosecution of inland discoveries. My
observations had been in a great measure confined to those points which curiosity, or a desire
of personal information, had prompted me to in-
vestigate. I did not, therefore, venture to flatter
myself that I had collected materials of sufficient
importance on general topics to enable me to write
for the information of others. Since my return
to England, however, I have been strenuously
urged to give a short description of the colony,
before entering upon my personal narrative ;
and I have conversed with so many individuals,
whose ideas of Australia are totally at variance
with its actual state, that I am encouraged to
indulge the hope that my observations, desultory

as they are, may be of some interest to the public. I am strengthened in this hope by the consideration that some kind friends have enabled me to add much valuable matter to that which I had myself collected. It is not my intention, however, to enter at any length on the commercial or agricultural interests of New South Wales. It may be necessary for me to touch lightly on those important subjects, but it is my wish to connect this preliminary chapter, as much as possible with the subjects treated of in the body of the work, and chiefly to notice the physical structure, the soil, climate, and productions of the colony, in order to convey to the reader general information on these points, before I lead him into the remote interior.

It may be worthy of remark, that the name " Australia," has of late years been affixed to that extensive tract of land which Great Britain possesses in the Southern Seas, and which, having been a discovery of the early Dutch navigators, was previously termed " New Holland." The change of name was, I believe, introduced by the celebrated French geographer, Malte Brun, who, in his division of the globe, gave the appel-

lation of Austral Asia and Polynesia to the new
discovered lands in the southern ocean; in which
division he meant to include the numerous insular
groups scattered over the Pacific.

Australia is properly speaking an island, but
it is so much larger than every other island on the
face of the globe, that it is classed as a continent,
in order to convey to the mind a just idea of its
magnitude. Stretching from the 115th to the 153d
degree of east longitude, and from the 10th to the
37th of south latitude, it averages 2700 miles in
length by 1800 in breadth; and, balanced, as it
were, upon the tropic of that hemisphere in which
it is situated, it receives the fiery heat of the equa-
tor at one extremity, while it enjoys the refreshing
coolness of the temperate zone at the other. On a
first view we should be led to expect that this
extensive tract of land possessed more than
ordinary advantages; that its rivers would be in
proportion to its size; and that it would abound
in the richest productions of the intertropical
and temperate regions. Such, indeed, was the
impression of those who first touched upon its
southern shores, but who remained no longer
than to be dazzled by the splendour and variety
of its botanical productions, and to enjoy for a

few days the delightful mildness of its climate. But the very spot which had appeared to Captain Cook and Sir Joseph Banks an earthly paradise, was abandoned by the early settlers as unfit for occupation; nor has the country generally been found to realize the sanguine expectations of those distinguished individuals, so far as it has hitherto been explored.

Rivers which have the widest mouths or the most practicable entrances, are, in Europe or America, usually of impetuous current, or else contain such a body of water as to bear down all opposition to their free course ; whilst, on the other hand, rivers whose force is expended ere they reach the sea, have almost invariably a bar at their embouchure, or where they mingle their waters with those of the ocean. This last feature unfortunately appears to characterize all the rivers of Australia, or such of them at least as are sufficiently known to us. Falling rapidly from the mountains in which they originate into a level and extremely depressed country ; having weak and inconsiderable sources, and being almost wholly unaided by tributaries of any kind; they naturally fail before they reach the coast, and exhaust themselves in marshes or lakes; or reach it so weakened as to be unable to preserve clear or navigable mouths, or to remove the sand banks that the tides throw up before them. On the other hand, the productions of this singular region seem to be peculiar to it, and unlike those of any other part of the world; nor have any indigenous fruits of any value as yet been found either in its forests or on its plains.

He who has never looked on any other than the well-cultured fields of England, can have little idea of a country that Nature has covered with an interminable forest. Still less can he estimate the feelings with which the adventurer approaches a shore that has never (or perhaps only lately) been trodden by civilized man.

It was with feelings peculiar to the occasion, that I gazed for the first time on the bold cliffs at the entrance of Port Jackson, as our vessel neared them, and speculated on the probable character of the landscape they hid; and I am free to confess, that I did not anticipate any thing equal to the scene which presented itself both to my sight and my judgment, as we sailed up the noble and extensive basin we had entered, towards the seat of government. A single glance was sufficient to tell me that the hills upon the southern shore of the port, the outlines of which were broken by houses and spires, must once have been covered with the same dense and gloomy wood which abounded every where else. The contrast was indeed very great — the improvement singularly striking. The labour and patience required, and the difficulties which the first settlers encountered in effecting these improvements, must have been incalculable. But their success has been complete: it is the very triumph of human skill and industry over Nature herself. The cornfield and the orchard have supplanted the wild grass and the brush; a flourishing town stands over the ruins of the forest; the lowing of herds has succeeded the wild whoop of the savage; and the stillness of that once desert shore is now broken by the sound of the bugle and the busy hum of commerce.

The Colony of New South Wales is situated upon the eastern coast of Australia; and the districts within which land has been granted to settlers, extends from the 36th parallel of latitude to the 32nd, that is say, from the

Moroyo River to the south of Sydney on the one hand, and to the Manning River on the other, including Wellington Valley within its limits to the westward. Thus it will appear that the boundaries of the located parts of the colony have been considerably enlarged, and some fine districts of country included within them. In consequence of its extent and increasing population, it has been found convenient to divide it into counties, parishes, and townships; and indeed, every measure of the Colonial Government of late years, has had for its object to assimilate its internal arrangements, as nearly as possible, to those of the mother country. Whether we are to attribute the present flourishing state of the colony to the beneficial influence of that system of government which has been exercised over it for the last seven years it is not for me to say. That the prosperity of a country depends, however, in a great measure, on the wisdom of its legislature, is as undoubted, as that within the period I have mentioned the colony of N. S. Wales has risen unprecedentedly in importance and in wealth, and has advanced to a state of improvement at which it could not have arrived had its energies been cramped or its interests neglected.

There is a period in the history of every country, during which it will appear to have been more prosperous than at any other. I allude not to the period of great martial achievements, should any such adorn its pages, but to that in which the enterprise of its merchants was roused into action, and when all classes of its community seem to have put forth their strength towards the attainment of wealth and power.

In this eventful period the colony of New South Wales is already far advanced. The conduct of its merchants is marked by the boldest speculations and the most gigantic projects. Their storehouses are built on the most magnificent scale, and with the best and most substantial materials. Few persons in England have even a remote idea of its present flourishing condition, or of the improvements that are daily taking place both in its commerce and in its agriculture. I am aware that many object to it as a place of residence, and I can easily enter into their feelings from the recollection of what my own were before I visited it. I cannot but remark, however, that I found my prejudices had arisen from a natural objection to the character of a part of its population ; from the circumstance of its being a penal colony, and from my total ignorance of its actual state, and not from any substantial or permanent cause. On the contrary I speedily became convinced of the exaggerated nature of the reports I had heard in England, on some of the points just adverted to ; nor did any thing fall under my observation during a residence in it of more than six years, to justify the opinion I had been previously led to entertain of it. I embarked for New South Wales, with strong prejudices against it: I left it with strong feelings in its favour, and with a deep feeling of interest in its prosperity. It is a pleasing task to me, therefore, to write of it thus, and to have it in my power to contribute to the removal of any erroneous impressions with regard to its condition at the present moment.

I have already remarked, that I was not prepared for the scene that met my view when I first saw Sydney. The fact was, I had not pictured to myself, nor conceived from any thing I had ever read or heard in England, that so extensive a town could have been reared in that remote region, in so brief a period as that which had elapsed since its foundation. It is not, however, a distant or cursory glance that will give the observer a just idea of the mercantile importance of this busy capital. In order to form an accurate estimate of it, he should take a boat and proceed from Sydney Cove to Darling Harbour. He would then be satisfied, that it is not upon the first alone that Australian commerce has raised its storehouses and wharfs, but that the whole extent of the eastern shore of the last more capacious basin, is equally crowded with warehouses, stores, dockyards, mills, and wharfs, the appearance and solidity of which would do credit even to Liverpool. Where, thirty years ago, the people flocked to the beach to hail an arrival, it is not now unusual to see from thirty to forty vessels riding at anchor at one time, collected there from every quarter of the globe. In 1831, one hundred and fifty vessels entered the harbour of Port Jackson, from foreign parts, the amount of their tonnage being 31,259 tons.

The increasing importance of Sydney must

in some measure be attributed to the flourishing condition of the colony itself, to the industry of its farmers, to the successful enterprise of its merchants, and to particular local causes. It is foreign to my purpose, however, to enter largely into an investigation of these important points. To do so would require more space than I can afford for the purpose, and might justly be considered as irrelevant in a work of this kind. Without attempting any lengthened detail, it may be considered sufficient if I endeavour merely to point out the principal causes of the present prosperity (and, as they may very probably prove) of the eventual progress of our great southern colony to power and independence.

The staple of our Australian colonies, but more particularly of New South Wales, the climate and the soil of which are peculiarly suited to its production,—is fine wool. There can be no doubt that the growth of this article has mainly contributed to the prosperity both of the above mentioned colony and of Van Dieman's Land.

At the close of the last century, wool was imported into England from Spain and Germany only, and but a few years previously from Spain

alone. Indeed, long after its introduction from
the latter country, German wool, obtained but
little consideration in the London market; and
in like manner, it may be presumed that many
years will not have elapsed before the increased
importation of wool from our own possessions in
the southern hemisphere, will render us, in respect
to this commodity, independent of every other
part of the world. The great improvements in
modern navigation are such, that the expence of
sending the fleece to market from New South
Wales, is less than from any part of Europe.
The charges for instance on Spanish and German wool, are from fourpence to fourpence three
farthings per pound ; whereas the entire charge,
after shipment from New South Wales, and Van
Dieman's Land, does not exceed threepence three
farthings, —and in this the dock and landing
charges, freight, insurance, brokerage, and com-
mission, are included.

As some particulars respecting the introduction of this source of national wealth into Australia, may prove interesting to the public, I have
put together the following details of it, upon the
authenticity of which they may rely. The person

who foresaw the advantage to be derived from the growth of fine wool in New South Wales, and who commenced the culture of it in that colony, was Mr. John M'Arthur. So far back, I believe, as the year 1793, not long after the establishment of the first settlement at Sydney, this gentleman commenced sheep-farming, and about two years afterwards he obtained a ram and two ewes from Captain Kent, of the royal navy, who had brought them, with some other stock for the supply of the settlement, from the Cape of Good Hope, to which place a flock of these sheep had been originally sent by the Dutch government. Sensible of the importance of the acquisition, Mr. M'Arthur began to cross his coarse-fleeced sheep with Merino blood ; and, proceeding upon a system, he effected a considerable improvement in the course of a few years. So prolific was this mixed breed, that in ten years, a flock which originally consisted of not more than seventy Bengal sheep, had increased in number to 4000 head, although the wethers had been killed as they became fit for slaughter. It appears, however, that as the sheep approached to greater purity of blood, their extreme fecundity diminished.

In 1803, Mr. M'Arthur revisited England; and there happening at the time to be a committee of manufacturers in London from the clothing districts, he exhibited before them samples of his wool, which were so much approved, that the committee represented to their constituents the advantages which would result from the growth of fine wool, in one of the southern dependencies of the empire. In consequence of this a memorial was transmitted to his Majesty's government, and Mr. M'Arthur's plans having been investigated by a Privy Council, at which he was present, they were recommended to the government as worthy of its protection. With such encouragement Mr. M'Arthur purchased two ewes and three rams, from the Merino flock of his Majesty King George the Third. He embarked with them on his return to New South Wales in 1806, on board a vessel named by him " the Argo," in reference to the golden treasure with which she was freighted. On reaching the colony he removed his sheep to a grant of land which the Home Government had directed he should receive in the Cow Pastures. To commemorate the transaction, and to transmit to a

grateful posterity the recollection of the noble-
man who then presided over the colonies, the
estate, together with the district in which it is
situated, was honoured by the name of Camden.

Since that time the value of New South Wales
wool has been constantly on the increase, and
the colony are indebted to Mr. M'Arthur for the
possession of an exportable commodity which
has contributed very materially to its present
wealth and importance. - Such general attention
is now paid to this interesting branch of rural
economy, that the importation of wool into England from our Australian colonies, amounted, in
1832, to 10,633 bales, or 2,500,000lbs. It has
been sold at as high a price as 10s. per lb.; but
the average price of wool of the best flocks vary
from 1s. 6d. to 4s. 6d. at the present moment. The
number of sheep in New South Wales alone was
calculated in the last census at 536,891 head.
The ordinary profits on this kind of stock may
be extracted from the Table given in the Ap-
pendix to the first volume of this work.

Among the various speculations undertaken
by the merchants of Sydney, there is not one
into which they have entered with so much

spirit as in the South Sea Fishery. The local situation of Port Jackson gives them an advantage over the English and the American merchants, since the distance of both these from the field of their gains, must necessarily impede them greatly; whereas the ships that leave Sydney on a whaling excursion, arrive without loss of time upon their ground, and return either for fresh supplies or to repair damages with equal facility. The spirit with which the colonial youth have engaged in this adventurous and hardy service, is highly to their credit. The profits arising from it may not be (indeed I have every reason to think are not) so great as might be supposed, or such as might reasonably be expected; but the extensive scale on which it is conducted, speaks equally for the energy and perseverance of the parties concerned, in the prosecution of their commercial enterprises. It has enabled them to equip a creditable colonial marine, and given great importance to their mercantile interests in the mother country.

In the year 1831, the quantity of sperm and black oil, the produce of the fisheries exported from New South Wales, amounted to 2307 tons, and was estimated, together with skins and whalebone, to be worth 107,971*l.* sterling. The gross amount of all other exports during that year, did not exceed 107,697*l.* sterling. Of these exports, the following were the most considerable :

Timber - - - -	£7,410
Butter and Cheese - - -	2,376
Mimosa bark - - -	40
Hides - - -- - -	7,333
Horses - - - - -	7,302
Salt provisions - - -	5,184
Wool - - -	66,112

The above is exclusive of £61,000 value of British manufactures re-exported to the various ports and islands in the Southern Seas.

In this scale, moreover, tobacco is not mentioned; but that plant is now raised for the supply of every private establishment, and will assuredly form an article of export, as soon as its manufacture shall be well understood. Neither can it be doubted but that the vine and the olive will, in a short time, be abundantly cultivated; and that a greater knowledge of the climate and soil of the more northern parts of the colony, will lead to the introduction of fresh sources of wealth.

Having taken this hasty review of the commercial interests of the colony, we may now turn to a brief examination of its internal structure and principal natural features.

I have already given a cursory sketch of the geographical features of the whole continent. Of the vast area which its coasts embrace, the east part alone has been fully explored.

A range of hills runs along the eastern coast, from north to south, which, in different quarters, vary in their distance from the sea; at one place approaching it pretty nearly, at another, receding from it to a distance of forty miles. It is a singular fact, that there is no pass or break in these mountains, by which any of the rivers of the interior can escape in an easterly direction. Their spine is unbroken. The consequence is, that there is a complete division of the eastern and western waters, and that streams, the heads of which are close to each other, flow away in opposite directions; the one to pursue a short course to the sea; the other to fall into a level and depressed interior, the character of which will be noticed in its proper place.

The proportion of bad soil to that which is good in New South Wales, is certainly very great: I mean the proportion of inferior soil to such as is fit for the higher purposes of agriculture. Mr. Dawson, the late superintendent of the Australian Agricultural Company's possessions, has observed, as a singular fact, that the best soil generally prevails on the summits of the hills, more especially where they are at all level. He accounts for so unusual a circumstance by the fact, that elevated positions are less subject to the effects of fire or floods than their valleys or flanks, and attributes the general want of vegetable mould over the colony chiefly to the ravages of the former element, whereby the growth of underwood, so favourable in other countries to the formation of soil, is wholly prevented. Undoubtedly this is a principal cause for the deficiency in question. There is no part of the world in which fires create such havoc as in New South Wales, and indeed in Australia generally. The climate, on the one hand, which dries up vegetation, and the wandering habits of the natives on the other, which induce them to clear the country before them by conflagration, operate equally against the growth of timber and underwood.

But there is another circumstance that appears to have escaped Mr. Dawson's observation; which is the actual property of the trees themselves, as to the quantity of vegetable matter they produce in decay. Being a military man, I cannot be supposed to have devoted much of my time to agricultural pursuits; but it has been obvious to me, as it must have been to many others, that in New South Wales, the fall of leaves and the decay of timber, so far from adding to the richness of its soil, actually destroy minor vegetation. This fact was brought more home to me in consequence of its having been my lot to spend some months upon Norfolk Island, a distant penal settlement attached to the Government of Sydney. There the abundance of vegetable decay was as remarkable as the want of it on the Australian Continent. I have frequently sunk up to my knees in a bed of leaves when walking through its woods; and,

often when I placed my foot on what appeared
externally to be the solid trunk of a tree, I have
found it yield to the pressure, in consequence of
its decomposition into absolute rottenness.   But
such is not the case in New South Wales. There,
no such accumulations of vegetable matter
are to be met with; but where the loftiest
tree of the forest falls to the ground, its figure
and length are marked out by the total want of
vegetation within a certain distance of it, and a
small elevation of earth, resembling more the
refuse or scoria of burnt bricks than any thing
else, is all that ultimately remains of the immense body which time or accident had pros-
trated. Thus it would appear, that it is not less
to the character of its woods than to the ravages
of fire that New South Wales owes its general
sterility.

Whilst prosecuting my researches in the interior of the colony, I could not but be struck
with the apparent connection between its geo-
logy and vegetation; so strong, indeed, was
this connection, that I had little difficulty, after
a short experience, in judging of the rock that
formed the basis of the country over which I

was travelling, from the kind of tree or herbage that flourished in the soil above it. The euca-lyptus pulv., a species of eucalyptus having a glaucus-coloured leaf, of dwarfish habits and growing mostly in scrub, betrayed the sand-stone formation, wherever it existed. This was the case in many parts of the County of Cum-berland, in some parts of Wombat Brush, at the two passes on the great south road, over a great extent of country to the N. W. of Yass Plains, and at Blackheath on the summit of the Blue Mountains. On the other hand, those open grassy and park-like tracts, of which so much has been said, characterise the secondary ranges of granite and porphyry. The trees most usual on these tracts, were the box, an unnamed species of eucalyptus, and the grass chiefly of that kind, called the oat or forest grass, which grows in tufts at considerable distances from each other, and which generally affords good pasturage. On the richer grounds the an-gophora lanceolata, and the eucalyptus mammi-fera more frequently point out the quality of the soil on which they grow. The first are abun-dant on the alluvial flats of the Nepean, the

Hawksbury and the Hunter; the latter on the limestone formation of Wellington Valley and in the better portions of Argyle; whilst the cupressus calytris seems to occupy sandy ridges with the casuarina. It was impossible that these broad features should have escaped observation: it was naturally inferred from this, that the trees of New South Wales are gregarious; and in fact they may, in a great measure, be considered so. The strong line that occasionally separates different species, and the sudden manner in which several species are lost at one point, to re-appear at another more distant, without any visible cause for the break that has taken place, will furnish a number of interesting facts in the botany of New South Wales.

It was observed both on the Macquarie river and the Morumbidgee, that the casuarinæ ceased at a particular point. On the Macquarie particularly, these trees which had often excited our admiration from Wellington Valley downwards, ceased to occupy its banks below the cataract, nor were they again noticed until we arrived on the banks of the Castlereagh. The blue-gum trees, again, were never observed to

extend beyond the secondary embankments of
the rivers, occupying that ground alone which
was subject to flood and covered with reeds.
These trees waved over the marshes of the Macquarie, but were not observed to the westward of
them for many miles ; yet they re-appeared upon
the banks of New-Year's Creek as suddenly as
they had disappeared after we left the marshes,
and grew along the line of the Darling to an
unusual size.   But it is remarkable, that, even
in the midst of the marshes, the blue-gum trees
were strictly confined to the immediate flooded
spaces on which the reeds prevailed, or to the
very beds of the water-courses.   Where the
ground was elevated, or out of the reach of flood,
the box (unnamed) alone occupied it ; and,
though the branches of these trees might be in-
terwoven together, the one never left its wet
and reedy bed, the other never descended from
its more elevated position.   The same singular
distinction marked the acacia pendula, when it
ceased to cover the interior plains of light earth,
and was succeeded by another shrub of the
same species.   It continued to the banks of New-
Year's Creek, a part of which it thickly lined.

To the westward of the creek, another species of acacia was remarked for the first time. Both shrubs, like the blue-gum and the box, mixed their branches together, but the creek formed the line of separation between them. The acacia pendula was not afterwards seen, but that which had taken its place, as it were, was found to cover large tracts of country and to form extensive brushes. Many other peculiarities in the vegetation of the interior are noticed in the body of this work, but I have thought that these more striking ones deserved to be particularly remarked upon.

If we strike a line to the N.W. from Sydney to Wellington Valley, we shall find that little change takes place in the geological features of the country. The sand-stone of which the first of the barrier ranges is composed, terminates a little beyond Mount York, and at Cox's River is succeeded by grey granite. The secondary ranges to the N.W. of Bathurst, are wholly of that primitive rock; for although there are partial changes of strata between Bathurst and Moulong Plains, granite is undoubtedly the rock upon which the whole are based: but at

Moulong Plains, a military station intermediate between Bathurst and Wellington Valley, limestone appears in the bed of a small clear stream, and with little interruption continues to some distance below the last-mentioned place. The accidental discovery of some caves at Moulong Plains, led to the more critical examination of the whole formation, and cavities of considerable size were subsequently found in various parts of it, but more particularly in the neighbourhood of Wellington Valley. The local interest which has of late years been taken in the prosecution of geological investigations, led many gentlemen to examine the contents of these caverns; and among the most forward, Major Mitchell, the Surveyor-General, must justly be considered, to whose indefatigable perseverance the scientific world is already so much indebted.

The caves into which I penetrated, did not present anything particular to my observation; they differed little from caves of a similar description into which I had penetrated in Europe. Large masses of stalactites hung from their roofs, and a corresponding formation encrusted their floors. They comprised various chambers or compartments, the most remote of which terminated at a deep chasm that was full of water. A close examination of these caves has led to the discovery of some organic remains, bones of various animals imbedded in a light red soil; but I am not aware that the remains of any extinct species have been found, or that any fossils have been met with in the limestone itself. There can, however, be little doubt but that the same causes operated in depositing these mouldering remains in the caves of Kirkdale and those of Wellington Valley.

About twenty miles below the junction of the Bell with the Macquarie, free-stone supersedes the limestone, but as the country falls rapidly from that point, it soon disappears, and the traveller enters upon a flat country of successive terraces. A schorl rock, of a blue colour and fine grain, composed of tourmaline and quartz, forms the bed of the Macquarie at the Cataract; and, in immediate contact with it, a mass of mica slate of alternate rose, pink, and white, was observed, which must have been covered by the waters of the river when Mr. Oxley descended it.

From the Cataract of the Macquarie, a flat extends to the marshes in which that river exhausts itself. From the midst of this flat Mount Foster and Mount Harris rise, both of which are porphyritic : but as I have been particular in describing these heights in their proper place, any minute notice of them here may be considered unnecessary. We will rather extend our enquiries to those parts of the colony upon which we shall not be called upon to remark in the succeeding pages.

Returning to the coast, we may mark the geological changes in a line to the S.W. of Sydney; and as my object is to extend the information of my readers, I shall notice any particular district on either side of the line I propose to touch upon, which may be worthy of notice. It would appear that the first decided break in the sandstone formation which penetrates into the county of Camden, is at Mittagong Range. It is there traversed by a dike of whinstone, of which that range is wholly composed. The change of soil and of vegetation are equally remarkable at this place ; the one being a rich, greasy, chocolate-coloured earth, the other partaking greatly of the intertropical character. In wandering over them, I noticed the wild fig and the cherry-tree, growing to a much larger size than I had seen them in any other part of the colony. Upon their branches, the satin bird, the gangan, and various kinds of pigeons were feeding. Birds unknown to the eastward of the Blue Mountains, were numerous in the valleys; and there was an unusual appearance of freshness and moisture in the vegetation.

These signs of improvement, however, vanish the moment Mittagong range is crossed, and sand-stone again forms the basis of the country to a considerable distance beyond Bong-bong. At a small farm called the Ploughed Ground, it is again traversed by a dike of whinstone, and a rich but isolated spot is thus passed over. With occasional and partial interruption, however, the sand-stone formation continues to an abrupt pass, from which the traveller descends to the county of Argyle. This pass is extremely abrupt, and is covered with glaucus, the low scrub I have noticed as common to the sand-stone formation. A small but lively stream, called Paddy's River, runs at the bottom of this pass,

and immediately to the S.W. of it, an open
forest country of granite base extends for many
miles, on which the eucalyptus manifera is prevalent, and which affords the best grazing tracts
in Argyle.   At Goulburn Plains, however, a
vein of limestone occurs, which is evidently connected with that forming the Shoal Haven Gully,
which is perhaps the most remarkable geological
feature in the colony of New South Wales.   It
is a deep chasm of about a quarter of a mile in
breadth, and 1200 feet in depth.   The country
on either side is perfectly level, so much so that
the traveller approaches almost to its very brink
before he is aware of his being near so singular
an abyss.   A small rivulet flows through the
Gully, and discharges itself into the sea at Shoal
Haven ; but this river is hardly perceptible, from
the summit of the cliffs forming the sides of the
Gully, which are of the boldest and most precipitous character.   The ground on the summit is
full of caves of great depth, but there has been
a difficulty in examining them, in consequence
of the violent wind that rushes up them, and ex-
tinguishes every torch.

The open and grassy forests of Argyle are terminated by another of those abrupt sand-stone passes I have just described, and the traveller again falls considerably from his former level, previously to his entering on Yass Plains, to which this pass is the only inlet.

From Yass Plains the view to the S. and S.W. is over a lofty and broken country : mountains with rounded summits, others with towering peaks, and others again of lengthened form but sharp spine, characterise the various rocks of which they are composed. The ranges decline rapidly from east to west, and while on the one hand the country has all the appearance of increasing height, on the other it sinks to a dead level ; nor on the distant horizon to the N. W. is there a hill or an inequality to be seen.

From Yass Plains to the very commencement of the level interior, every range I crossed presented a new rock-formation ; serpentine quartz in huge white masses, granite, chlorite, micaceous schist, sandstone, chalcedony, quartz, and red jasper, and conglomerate rocks.

It was however, out of my power, in so hurried a journey as that which I performed down the banks of the Morumbidgee River, to examine, with the accuracy I could have wished, either the immediate connection between these rocks or their gradual change from the one to the other. I was content to ascertain their actual succession, and to note the general outlines of the ranges; but the defect of vision under which I labour, prevents me from laying them before the public.

From what has been advanced, however, it will appear that the physical structure of the southern parts of the colony is as varied, as that of the western interior is monotonous, and we may now pursue our original observations on the soil of the colony with greater confidence.

In endeavouring to account for the poverty of the soil in New South Wales, and in attributing it in a great degree to the causes already mentioned, it appears necessary to estimate more specifically the influence which the geological formation of a country exercises on its soil, and how much the quality of the latter partakes of the character of the rock on which it reposes. And although I find it extremely difficult to explain myself as I should wish to do, in the critical discussion on which I have thus entered, yet as it is material to the elucidation of an important subject in the body of the work, I feel it incumbent on me to proceed to the best of my ability.

I have said that the soil of a country depends much upon its geological formation. This appears to be particularly the case in those parts of the colony with which I am acquainted, or those lying between the parallels of 30° and 35° south. Sandstone, porphyry, and granite, succeed each other from the coast to a very considerable distance into the interior, on a N. W. line. The light ferruginous dust that is distributed over the county of Cumberland, and which annoys the traveller by its extreme minuteness, to the eastward of the Blue Mountains, is as different from the coarse gravelly soil on the secondary ranges to the westward of them, as the barren scrubs and thickly-wooded tracts of the former district are to the grassy and open forests of the latter.

As soon as I began to descend to the westward, it became necessary to pay strict and earnest attention to the features of the country through which I passed, in order to determine more accurately the different appearances which, as I was led to expect, the rivers would assume. In the course of my examination I found, first, that the broken country through which I travelled, was generally covered with a loose, coarse, and sandy soil; and, secondly, that the ranges were wholly deficient in that peat formation which fills the valleys, or covers the flat summits of the hills or mountains, in the northern hemisphere. The peculiar property of this formation is to retain water like a sponge; and to this property the regular and constant flow of the rivers descending from such hills, may, in a great measure, be attributed. In New South Wales, on the contrary, the rains that fall upon the mountains drain rapidly through a coarse and superficial soil, and pour down their sides without a moment's interruption. The consequence is that on such occasions the rivers are subject to great and sudden rises, whereas they have scarcely water enough to support a current in ordinary seasons. At one time the traveller will find it impracticable to cross them: at another he may do so with ease; and

only from the remains of debris in the branches
of the trees high above, can he judge of the
furious torrent they must occasionally contain.

This seeming deviation on the part of Nature
from her usual laws will no longer appear such,
if we consider its results for a moment. The
very floods which swell the rivers to overflowing,
are followed by the most beneficent effects ; and,
rude and violent as the means are by which she
accomplishes her purpose, they form, no doubt,
a part of that process by which she preserves
the balance of good and evil. Vast quantities of
the best soil have been thus washed down from the
mountains to accumulate in more accessible
places. From frequent depositions, a great extent of country along the banks of every river
and creek has risen high above the influence of
the floods, and constitutes the richest tracts in
the colony. The alluvial flats of the Nepean,
the Hawksbury, and the Hunter, are striking
instances of the truth of these observations ; to
which the plains of O'Connel and Bathurst may
be added. The only good soil upon the two
latter, is in the immediate neighbourhood of the
Macquarie River : but, even close to its banks,

the depositions are of little depth, lying on a coarse gravelly soil, the decomposition of the nearer ranges. The former is found to diminish in thickness, according to the concavity of the valley through which the Macquarie flows, and at length becomes mixed with the coarser soil. This deposit is alone fit for agricultural purposes; but it does not necessarily follow that the distant country is unavailable, since it is admitted, that the best grazing tracts are upon the secondary ranges of granite and porphyry. These ranges generally have the appearance of open forest, and are covered with several kinds of grasses, among which the long oat-grass is the most abundant.

If we except the valley of the Nepean, the banks of the South Creek, the Pennant Hills near Paramatta, and a few other places, the general soil of the county of Cumberland, is of the poorest description. It is superficial in most places, resting either upon a cold clay, or upon sandstone; and is, as I have already remarked, a ferruginous compound of the finest dust. Yet there are many places upon its surface, (hollows for instance,) in which vegetable decay has accumulated, or valleys, into which it has been washed, that are well adapted for the usual purposes of agriculture, and would, if the country was more generally cleared, be found to exist to a much greater extent than is at present imagined. I have frequently observed these isolated patches of better land, when wandering through the woods, both on the Paramatta River, and at a greater distance from the coast. And I cannot but think, that it would be highly advantageous to those who possess large properties in the County of Cumberland to let portions of them. The concentration of people round their capital, promotes more than anything else the prosperity of a colony, by creating a reciprocal demand for the produce both of the country and the town, since the one would necessarily stimulate the energy of the farmer, as the other would rouse the enterprise of the merchant. The consideration, however, of such a subject is foreign to my present purpose.

It must not be supposed, that because I have given a somewhat particular description of the County of Cumberland, I have done so with a view to bring it forward as a specimen of the other counties, or to found upon it a general description of the colony. It is, in fact, poorer in every respect than any tract of land of similar extent in the interior, and is still covered with dense forests of heavy timber, excepting where the trees have been felled by dint of manual labour, and the ground cleared at an expence that nothing but its proximity to the seat of government could have justified. But experience has proved, that neither the labour nor the expence have been thrown away. Many valuable farms and extensive gardens checquer the face of the country, from which the proprietors derive a very efficient income.

To the westward of the Blue Mountains, the country differs in many respects from that lying between those ranges and the coast; and, although, its aspect varies in different places, three principal features appear more immediately to characterise it. These are, first, plains of considerable extent wholly destitute of timber; secondly, open undulating woodlands; and, thirdly, barren unprofitable tracts. The first almost invariably occur in the immediate neighbourhood of some river, as the Plains

of Bathurst, which are divided by the Macquarie; Goulburn Plains, through which the Wal-
landilly flows; and Yass Plains, which are watered by a river of the same name.   The open forests, through which the horseman may gallop
in perfect safety, seem to prevail over the whole
secondary ranges of granite, and are generally
considered as excellent grazing tracts.   Such is
the country in Argyleshire on either side of the
Lachlan, where that river crosses the great southern road near Mr. Hume's station; such also are
many parts of Goulburn, and the whole extent of
country lying between Underaliga and the Morumbidgee River.   The barren tracts, on the
other hand, may be said to occupy the central
spaces between all the principal streams.   With
regard to the proportion that these different
kinds of country bear to each other, there can be
no doubt of the undue preponderance of the last
over the first two; but there are nevertheless
many extensive available tracts in every part of
the colony.

. The greatest disadvantage under which New
South Wales labours, is the want of means for
conveying inland produce to the market, or to the

coast. The Blue Mountains are in this respect
a serious bar to the internal prosperity of the colony. By this time, however, a magnificent road
will have been completed across them to the
westward, over parts of which I travelled in 1831.
Indeed the efforts of the colonial government
have been wisely directed, not only to the construction of this road, which the late Governor,
General Darling commenced, but also in facilitat-
ing the communication to the southern districts,
by an almost equally fine road over the Razor
Back Range, near the Cow Pastures ; so that as
far as it is possible for human efforts to overcome
natural obstacles, the wisdom and foresight of the
executive have ere this been successful.

The majority of the settlers in the Bathurst
country, and in the more remote interior, are wool
growers ; and as they send their produce to the
market only once a year, receiving supplies for
home consumption, on the return of their drays
or carts from thence, the inconvenience of bad
roads is not so much felt by them. But to an
agriculturist, a residence to the westward of
the Blue Mountains is decidedly objectionable,
unless he possess the means with which to pro-

cure the more immediate necessaries of life, otherwise than by the sale of his grain or other produce, and can be satisfied to cultivate his property for home consumption, or for the casual wants of his neighbours. Under such circumstances, a man with a small private income would enjoy every rational comfort. But of course, not only in consequence of the loss of labour, but the chance of accidents during a long journey, the more the distance is increased from Sydney, as the only place at which the absolute necessaries of life can be purchased, the greater becomes the objection to a residence in such a part of the country; and on this account it is, that although some beautiful locations both as to extent and richness, are to be found to the westward of Bathurst, equally on the Bell, the Macquarie, and the Lachlan, it is not probable they will be taken up for many years, or will only be occupied as distant stock stations.

Since, therefore, it appears from what has been advanced, that it is not to the westward the views of any settlers should be directed, excepting under particular circumstances, it remains for us to consider what other parts of the colony hold out, or appear to hold out, greater advantages. The eye naturally turns to the south on the one hand, and to Port-Macquarie northerly on the other. It is to be remarked that the eastern shores of Australia partake of the same barren character that marks the other three. It is generally bounded to a certain extent by a sandy and sterile tract. There are, however, breaks in so prolonged a line, as might have been expected, where, from particular local causes, both the soil and vegetation are of a superior kind. At Illawarra for instance, the contiguity of the mountains to the coast leaves no room for the sandy belt we have noticed, but the debris from them reaches to the very shore. Whether from reflected heat, or from some other peculiarity of situation, the vegetation of Illawarra is of an intertropical character, and birds that are strangers to the county of Cumberland frequent its thickets. There is no part of Australia where the feathered race are more beautiful, or more diversified. The most splendid pigeon, perhaps, that the world produces, and the satin bird, with its lovely eye, feed there upon the berries of the ficus (wild fig,) and other trees: and a numerous tribe of the accipitrine class soar over its dense and spacious forests.

We again see a break in the sandy line of the coast at Broken Bay, at Newcastle, and still further north at Port Macquarie; at which places the Hawkesbury, the Hunter, and the Hastings severally debouche. Of Port Macquarie, as a place of settlement, I entertain a very high opinion, in consequence of its being situated under a most favourable parallel of latitude. I am convinced it holds out many substantial advantages. One of the most important of these is the circumstance of its having been much improved when occupied as a penal settlement. And since the shores of the colony are now navigated by steamboats, the facility of water communication would be proportionably great.

I believe the Five Islands or Illawarr district is considered peculiarly eligible for small settlers. The great drawback to this place is the heavy character of its timber and the closeness of its thickets, which vie almost with the American woods in those respects. The return, however, is adequate to the labour required in clearing the ground. Between the Five Islands and

Sydney, a constant intercourse is kept up by numerous small craft; and a communication with the interior, by branch roads from the great southern line to the coast, would necessarily be thrown open, if the more distant parts of it were sufficiently peopled.

Recent surveys have discovered to us rich and extensive tracts in the remote interior between Jervis Bay and Bateman's Bay, and southwards upon the western slope of the dividing range. The account given by Messrs. Hovel and Hume is sufficient to prove that every valley they crossed was worthy of notice, and that the several rivers they forded were flanked by rich and extensive flats.

The distance of Moneroo Plains, and of the Doomot and Morumbidgee Rivers from Sydney, alarms the settler, who knows not the value of those localities; but men whose experience has taught them to set this obstacle at nought, have long depastured their herds on the banks of the last two. The fattest cattle that supply the Sydney market are fed upon the rich flats, and in the grassy valleys of the Morumbidgee; and there are several beautiful farms upon those of the Doomot. Generally speaking, the persons who reside in those distant parts, pay little attention to the comfort of their dwellings, or to the raising of more grain than their establishments may require; but there can be no doubt this part of the interior ought to be the granary of New South Wales; its climate and greater humidity being more favourable than that of Sydney for the production of wheat.

The most serious disadvantage under which the colony of New South Wales labours, is in the drought to which it is periodically subject. Its climate may be said to be too dry; in other respects it is one of the most delightful under heaven; and experience of the certainty of the recurrence of the trying seasons to which I allude, should teach men to provide against their effects. Those seasons, during which no rain falls, appear, from the observations of former writers, to occur every ten or twelve years; and it is somewhat singular that no cause has been assigned for such periodical visitations. Whether the state of the interior has anything to do with them, and whether the wet or dry condition of the marshes at all regulate the seasons, is a question upon which I will not venture to give any decisive opinion. But most assuredly, when the interior is dry, the seasons are dry, and *vice versa*. Indeed, not only is this the case, but rains, from excessive duration in the first year after a drought, decrease gradually year after year, until they wholly cease for a time. It seems not improbable, therefore, that the state of the interior does, in some measure, regulate the fall of rain upon the eastern ranges, which appears to decrease in quantity yearly as the marshes become exhausted, and cease altogether, when they no longer contain any water. A drought will naturally follow until such time as the air becomes surcharged with clouds or vapour from the ocean, which being no longer able to sustain their own weight, descend upon the mountains, and being conveyed by hundreds of streams into the western lowlands, again fill the marshes, and cause the recurrence of regular seasons.

The thermometer ranges during the summer months, that is, from September to March, from 36° to 106° of Fahrenheit, but the mean of the temperature during the above period is 70°.

The instrument in the winter months ranges from 27° to 98°, with a mean of 66°. However great the summer heat may appear, it is certain that the climate of New South Wales has not the relaxing and enfeebling effect upon the constitution, which renders a residence in India or other parts of the south so intolerable. Neither are any of the ordinary occupations of business or of pleasure laid aside at noon, or during the hottest part of the day. The traveller may cast himself at length under the first tree that invites him, and repose there as safely as if he were in a palace. Fearless of damps, and unmolested by noxious insects, his sleep is as sound as it is refreshing, and he rises with renewed spirits to pursue his journey. Equally so may the ploughman or the labourer seek repose beside his team, and allow them to graze quietly round him. The delicious coolness of the morning and the mild temperature of the evening air, in that luxurious climate, are beyond the power of description. It appears to have an influence on the very animals, the horses and and cattle being particularly docile; and I cannot but think it has in some degree the same happy effect upon some of the hardened human beings who are sent thither from the old world.

As I have before observed, it has not yet been discovered whether there are any indigenous fruits of any value in Australia. In the colony of New South Wales there certainly are none; yet the climate is peculiarly adapted for the growth of every European and of many tropical productions. The orange, the fig, the citron, the pomegranate, the peach, the apple, the guava, the nectarine, the pear, and the loquette, grow side by side together. The plantain throws its broad leaves over the water, the vine encircles the cottages, and the market of Sydney is abundantly supplied with every culinary vegetable.

In a climate, therefore, so soft that man scarcely requires a dwelling, and so enchanting that few have left it but with regret, the spirits must necessarily be acted upon, — and the heart feel lighter. Such, indeed, I have myself found to be the case; nor have I ever been happier that when roving through the woods or wandering along one of the silent and beautiful bays for which the harbour of Port Jackson is so celebrated. I went to New South Wales as I have already remarked, highly prejudiced against it, both from the nature of the service, and the character of the great body of its inhabitants. My regiment has since quitted its shores, but I am aware there are few of them who would not gladly return. The feeling I have in its favour arises not, therefore, from the services in which I was employed, but from circumstances in the colony itself; and I yet hope to form one of its community, and to join a number of valuable and warm-hearted friends whom I left in that distant part of the world.

On the subject of emigration, it is not my intention to dwell at any length. My object in these preliminary remarks has been to give the reader a general idea of the country, into the interior recesses of which I am about to lead him. Still, however, it may be useful to offer a few general observations on a topic which has, of late years, become so interesting to the British public.

The main consideration with those who, possessing some capital, propose to emigrate as the means of improving their condition, is, the society likely to be found in the land fixed on for their future residence. One of the first questions I have been asked, when conversing on the subject of emigration, has consequently related to this important matter. I had only then to observe in reply, that the civil and military establishments in New South Wales, form the elements of as good society as it is the lot of the majority to command in Great Britain.

The houses of the settlers are not scattered over a greater surface than the residences of country gentlemen here, and if they cannot vie with them in size, they most assuredly do in many other more important respects; and if a substantial cottage of brick or stone has any claim to the rank of a tenantable mansion, there are few of them which do not possess all the means of exercising that hospitality for which young communities are remarkable.

But to sever the links of kindred, and to abandon the homes of our fathers after years of happy tranquillity, is a sacrifice the magnitude of which is unquestionable. The feelings by which men are influenced under such circumstances have a claim to our respect. Indeed, no class of persons can have a stronger hold upon our sympathies than those whom unmerited adverse fortune obliges to seek a home in a distant country.

Far, therefore, be it from me to dispute a single expression of regret to which they may give utterance. It must, however, be remembered that the deepest feelings of anguish are providentially alleviated in time. Our heaviest misfortunes are frequently repaired by industry and caution. The sky clears up, as it were: new interests engage the attention, and the cares of a family or the improvement of a newly acquired property engross those moments which would otherwise be spent in vain and unprofitable regrets.

It cannot be doubted that persons such as I have described, whose conduct has hitherto been regulated by prudence, and whose main object is to provide for their children, are the most valuable members of every community, whether young or old. To such men few countries hold out greater prospects of success than New South Wales; for the more we extend our enquiries, the more we shall find that the success of the emigrant in that colony depends upon his prudence and foresight rather than on any collateral circumstance of climate or soil; and to him who can be satisfied with the gradual acquirement of competency, it is the land of promise. Blessed with a climate of unparalleled serenity, and of unusual freedom from disease, the settler has little external cause of anxiety, little apprehension of sickness among his family or domestics, and little else to do than to attend to his own immediate interests. 1 should wish to illustrate the observations by two or three instances of their practical bearing and tendency.

It was on my return from my second expedition, that I visited Lieut. * * * * * * who resides in the southern parts of the colony. The day after my arrival, he took me round his property, and explained the various improvements he had made, considering the small means with which he had commenced. At this part of our conversation, we came within view of his house, a substantial weather-board cottage. " I trust," said I, turning to him, "you will excuse the question I am about to ask ; for your frankness emboldens me to propose it, and on your answer much of the effect of what you have been saying will depend. In effecting these various improvements, and in the building of that house, have you been obliged to embarrass yourself, or are they free from incumbrance ?" — " Your question," he said, " is a reasonable one, and I will answer it with the frankness you are kind

enough to ascribe to me. I have ever made it
a rule not to exceed my income. Mrs. * * *
*. * * bore our first trials with so much cheer-
fulness, and contributed so much to my happi-
ness and my prosperity, that I felt myself bound
to build her a good house with the first money
I had to spare." I confess this answer raised my
host in my estimation, and it was a gratifying
proof to me of the success that attends industry
and perseverance.

But let us look at another case. Mr. * * * had
a property to the N.W. of Sydney, and having
considerable funded means when he arrived in
the colony, he soon put his property into a state of
progressive improvement, and being in truth an
excellent practical farmer, it assumed the appearance of regularity and order. Had Mr. * * * stopped at this moment, he would have been in the en-
joyment of affluence and of every rational comfort.
But instead of exercising prudent rules of hospitality, he gave way to the natural generosity of
his disposition, entered into expences he could
not afford, and was ultimately obliged to part
with his estate. Now it is deeply to be regretted,
that one whose energies and abilities particularly
fitted him for the life he had chosen, should have

failed through such conduct; and it is more than probable, that if he had commenced with smaller means, and had gradually improved his property, his fate would have been very different.

I shall leave these cases without any further comment, convinced as I am, that each of them furnishes matter for serious consideration, and that they are practical illustrations of the causes of success or failure of those who emigrate to the colony of New South Wales. And although I do not mean to affirm, that the majority follow Mr. * * *'s example, I must venture to assert that thoughtlessness—useless expenditure in the first instance—waste of time and other circumstances, lead to equally ruinous consequences.

One of the greatest objections which families have to New South Wales, is their apprehension of the moral effects that are likely to overwhelm them by bad example, and for which no success in life could compensate. In a colony constituted like that of New South Wales, the proportion of crime must of course be great. Yet it falls less under the notice of private families than one might at first sight have been led to suppose. Drunkenness, as in the mother

country, is the besetting sin; but it is confined
chiefly to the large towns in consequence of the
difficulty of procuring spirits in the country.
There are, no doubt, many incorrigible characters sent to settle in the interior, and it is an evil
to have these men, even for a single day, to break
the harmony of a previously well regulated establishment, or to injure its future prospects by
the influence of evil example. They are men
who are sent upon trial, from on board a newly
arrived ship, and they generally terminate their
misconduct either on the roads or at a penal
settlement, being thus happily removed from the
mass of the prisoners. Frequently, however, men
remain for years under the same master. They
become attached to their occupations, their
hearts become softened by kindness, and they
atone as much as they possibly can for previous
error.

Still there can be no doubt, but that the evil
complained of is considerable. It is from this
reason, and from my personal knowledge of the
southern parts of the colony, that I should re-
joice to see its flats and its valleys filled with an
industrious population of a better description of
farmers. A hope might then be reasonably in-

dulged, that the Home Government would not
be backward in recognising, and in acting upon
a principle, the soundness of which has been felt
and acknowledged in all ages, but the chief difficulty of which rests in its judicious application.
I allude to a system of emigration. Sure I am
that if it were well organized, and care were
taken to profit by the experience of the past in
similar attempts, it could not fail to be attended
with ultimate success. The evils resulting from
a surplus population in an old community, were
never more seriously felt than in Great Britain
at the present moment. Assuming that the
amount of surplus population is 2,000,000, the
excess of labour and competition thus occasioned,
by diminishing profits and wages, creates, it has
been said, an indirect tax to the enormous extent
of 20,000,000l. per annum. It has appeared to
many experienced persons, that it is in emigration, we should best find the means of relief from
this heavy pressure; particularly if the individuals encouraged to go out to the colonies were
young persons of both sexes, from the industrious
classes of the community. Even if no more than
three couples were induced to emigrate from each
parish in England in ten years, the relief to the

springs of industry would be very great. Besides, the funds necessary for this purpose would revert to the country by a thousand indirect channels. Persons unacquainted with our Australian colonies, whether Van Dieman's Land or New South Wales, can form little idea of the increasing demand for, and consumption in them of every species of British manufacture. The liberal encouragement given by government to every practicable scheme of emigration, and the sum advanced by it towards the expences of the voyage to the labouring classes, sufficiently indicate the light in which the subject is viewed by the legislature; and the fact that no private family taking out servants to Sydney, has in any one instance been able to retain them, on account of offers more advantageous from other quarters, shews clearly the great demand for labour in the colony. If I might judge of the feelings of the majority of respectable individuals there, from the assurances of the few, they would willingly defray any parochial expences attendant on the voyage, provided the services of such individuals could be secured to them for a time sufficiently long to remunerate them for such payment. The tide of emigration should be directed to Sydney, Van Dieman's

Land, or Western Australia, upon condition of
the labourer's receiving a certain sum in wages,
and his daily subsistence from his employer, with
an understanding, however, that he must consider
himself bound for two years to such employer.
Surely there are hundreds of our indigent coun-
trymen, who would gladly seek a land of such
plenty, and cast away the natural, but unavail-
ing regret of leaving home to secure to themselves and their families, the substantial comforts of life on such easy conditions.

It is not, perhaps, generally known that a
committee has been formed in Sydney, to advise settlers as to the best mode of proceeding
on arrival there. Such a plan is one of obvious
utility; and if those who may find themselves at
a loss for information would apply to this committee for advice, rather than to individuals
with whom they may become casually acquainted,
they would further their own interests, and in all
probability ensure success. Still there are some
broad rules upon which every man ought to act,
which I shall endeavour to point out, and it will
give me no ordinary satisfaction, if I should be
the means of directing any one to the road of
prosperity and comfort.

It is to be feared that those who emigrate to New South Wales, generally anticipate too great facility in their future operations and certainty of success in conducting them ; but they should recollect that competency cannot be obtained without labour. Every trade—every profession, in this respect, is subject to the same law — the lawyer, the physician, the tradesman, and the mechanic. This labour is required at our hands, even in an old community; how much more then is it called for in a new, where the ingenuity of men is put to trial to secure those means of accomplishing their ends which here are abundant. Now, it appears to me but consistent, that he who is obliged to leave his native country from want of means to hold his station there, can hardly expect to find, or rather to secure, abundance elsewhere without some exertion. Every man who emigrates should proceed with a conviction on his mind, that he is about to encounter years of labour and privation. He will not then be disappointed at partial reverses, and will be more thankful for unexpected prosperity. I feel persuaded the tone of mind has a great deal to do with success, because it influences the conduct of the individual. Supposing, however, that an emigrant has taken this rational view of his situation, he should determine on his pursuits, and allow nothing but absolute certainty of better fortune to turn him aside. Men, however, landing at Sydney, in their eagerness for information get bewildered, give up their original plans, adopt new and uncertain speculations, trifle away both their time and their money, and ultimately ruin themselves. An individual who goes to New South Wales for the purpose of settling, should not remain in Sydney a day longer than is necessary for the arrangement of his affairs. Every shilling spent there is thrown away. The greatest facility is given by the different departments of the Colonial Government to the settlers; and it is entirely his own fault if he trifles away his time in search of information elsewhere than at the fountain-head, or if he trusts to any other opinion than his own, supposing him experienced as to the quality of the land he may fix upon. Let him be speedy in his selection, and fix himself upon his allotment as soon as possible. Instead of overstocking his farm, or employing more labourers than he can afford to keep, let him be satisfied with a gradual increase of his stock, and wait patiently till he can better afford to employ labour; above all, let him avoid embarrassing himself by the purchase of any superfluous or unnecessary comfort. I consider that man has already failed, who runs into debt in the first instance, or who exhausts his means in the purchase of large herds, from the vain expectation that their increase will clear him. The time was when those idle speculations were occasionally attended with success, but such is not now the case. The energies of the agriculturist are directed to their proper channel, and if the few are unable to make rapid fortunes, the many have escaped inevitable ruin. No farm in a state of nature can be expected to yield any return of consequence for the first year. It is incumbent on a settler to provide for his establishment, or to retain the means of providing for it as circumstances may require.

Farming implements are as cheap in Sydney as in England. Horses and cattle are cheaper. It requires little, therefore, to stock a farm in a reasonable manner. On the other hand, the climate is so mild that the want of a house is scarcely felt, and a temporary residence easily constructed. On the whole I am convinced, that a man who regulates his conduct by prudence, and who perseveringly follows up his occupations, who behaves with kindness to those around him, and performs his social and moral duties with punctuality, will ultimately secure to himself a home that will make up for the one he has quitted in the land of his fathers, and place him in as respectable and as happy a situation as that which he there enjoyed.

———

Having thrown out the foregoing remarks for the information of the general reader, and of persons who look to Australia with the more earnest views of selecting a colonial home, I now return to the immediate object of these volumes ; but before entering on the narrative of my own expeditions, I think it necessary to advert cursorily to the discoveries previously accomplished.

The journeys of Mr. Oxley, far into the western interior of Australia, gave rise to various and conflicting opinions as to the character of the more central parts of that extensive continent, of which the colony of New South Wales forms but a small portion. I feel, therefore, called upon briefly to advert to the con-

clusions which that able and intelligent officer
drew from his personal observation of the country into which he penetrated, as an acquaintance
with his opinions will not only tend to throw a
clearer light on the following details, but will,
also, convey much necessary information to those
of my readers who may not have perused his
journals. It is necessary, however, in order to
divest the subject of all obscureness, to trace,
in the first instance, the progress of inland discovery, in New South Wales, from the first
foundation of the colony to the period when Mr.
Oxley's exertions attracted the public attention.

In the year 1788, the British Government
took formal possession of the eastern coast of
Australia, by the establishment of a penal colony at Port Jackson. The first settlers, under
Governor Phillips, had too many difficulties to
contend with to submit themselves to be thwart-
ed from pursuits essential to their immediate
safety and comfort, by the prospect of remote
and uncertain advantages. It was by perseverance and toil alone that they first established
and ultimately spread themselves over that part
of the territory, which, flanked by the ocean on
the one hand, and embraced as it were by the

Nepean River on the other, is now entitled the County of Cumberland. For many years, this single district supplied the wants of the settlers. Upon it they found ample pasture for their herds, and sufficient employment for themselves. Nor was it until a succession of untoward seasons, and the rapid increase of their stock pointed out to them the necessity of seeking for more extensive pasturage, that they contemplated surmounting that dark and rugged chain of mountains, which, like the natural ramparts of Spain and Italy, rose high over the nether forest, and broke the line of the western horizon.

A Mr. Caley is said to have been the first who attempted to scale the Blue Mountains: but he did not long persevere in struggling with difficulties too great for ordinary resolution to overcome. It appears that he retraced his steps, after having penetrated about sixteen miles into their dark and precipitous recesses; and a heap of stones, which the traveller passes about that distance from Erne Ford, on the road to Bathurst, marks the extreme point reached by the first expedition to the westward of the Nepean river.

Shortly after the failure of this expedition, the sad effects of a long protracted drought called forth a more general spirit of enterprise and exertion among the settlers; and Mr. Oxley makes honorable mention of the perseverance and resolution with which Lieut. Lawson, of the 104th regiment, accompanied by Messrs. Blaxland and Wentworth, conducted an expedition into the Blue Mountains. Their efforts were successful: and the objects of their enterprise would have been completely attained, but for the failure of their provisions at a moment when their view of the distant interior was such as to convince them that they had overcome the most formidable obstacles to their advance, and that in their further progress few impediments would have presented themselves.

The success of this undertaking induced Governor Macquarie to further the prosecution of inland discovery, and of attempts to ascertain the nature of the country of which Mr. Lawson only obtained a glimpse. An expedition was accordingly dispatched under Mr. Evans, the Deputy Surveyor-General, to follow the route taken by the former one, and to penetrate as far as practicable into the western interior. The result was the discovery of the Macquarie river, and of Bathurst Plains. The report of Mr.

Evans was so favourable, that orders were immediately issued for the construction of a line of road across the mountains. When that was completed, the Governor went in person to fix the site of a future town on Bathurst Plains. From thence Mr. Evans, who accompanied the Governor on the occasion, was directed to proceed to the southward and westward, to ascertain the nature of the country in that direction. He discovered another considerable river, flowing, like the Macquarie, to the west, to which he gave the name of the Lachlan. The promising appearance of these two streams, and the expectation of all parties that they would be found to water rich and extensive tracts of country, led to the fitting out of a more important expedition than any which had before been contemplated.

Mr. Oxley, the Surveyor-General of the Colony, was appointed chief of this expedition, and was directed to trace the Lachlan and Macquarie rivers, as far as practicable, with a view to ascertain their capabilities and the nature of the country they watered. In 1817, Mr. Oxley directed his attention to the former river, and continued to follow its windings, until it appeared that its waters were lost in successive marshes and it ceased to be a river. In the following year he turned towards the Macquarie, and traced it, in like manner, until he was checked by high reeds that covered an extensive plain before him, amidst which the channel of the river was lost.

From what he observed of the country, on both these occasions, he was led to infer that beyond the limits of his advance the interior had a uniform level, and was, for the most part, uninhabitable and under water. Its features must have been strongly marked to have confirmed such an opinion in the mind of the late Surveyor-General. It stands recorded on the pages of his journal, that he travelled over a country of many miles in extent, after clearing the mountains, which so far from presenting any rise of ground to the eye, bore unequivocal marks of frequent and extensive inundation. He traced two rivers of considerable size, and found that, at a great distance from each other, they apparently terminated in marshes, and that the country beyond them was low and unbroken. In his progress eastward, he crossed a third stream (the Castlereagh), about forty-five miles

from the Macquarie, seemingly not inferior to it
in size, originating in the mountains for which
he was making, and flowing nearly parallel to
the other rivers into a level country like that
which he had just quitted.

Mr. Evans, moreover, who accompanied Mr.
Oxley on these journeys, and who had been
detached by his principal from Mount Harris, to
ascertain the nature of the country in the line
which the expedition was next to pursue, having
crossed the Castlereagh considerably below the
place at which the party afterwards effected a
passage, reported that the river was then running through high reeds. The inference naturally drawn by Mr. Oxley, was, that it terminated as the Lachlan and the Macquarie had
done; and that their united waters formed an
inland sea or basin. It is evident that Mr.
Oxley had this impression on his mind, when
he turned towards the coast; but the wet state
of the lowlands prevented him from ascertaining
its correctness or error. Doubt, consequently,
still existed as to the nature of the country he
had left behind him; a question in which the best
interests of the colony were apparently involved.
Subsequently to these discoveries, Mr. Surveyor

Mechan, accompanied by Mr. Hamilton Hume, a colonist of considerable experience, explored the country more to the southward and westward of Sydney, and discovered most of the new country called Argyle, and also Lake Bathurst.

Mr. Hume was afterwards associated with a Mr. Hovel, in an excursion to the south coast, under the auspices of Sir Thomas Brisbane. After a most persevering and laborious journey, they reached the sea; but it is uncertain whether they made Port Philips, or Western Port. Mr. Hume, whose practical experience will yield to that of no man, entertains a conviction that it was to the former they descended from the neighbouring ranges; but Mr. Hovel, I believe, supports a contrary opinion. In the early stage of their journey, they passed over York or Yass Plains; and, after crossing the Morumbidgee, were generally entangled among mountain ranges that increased in height to the east and southeast. They crossed three considerable rivers, falling westerly, which they named the Goulburn, the Hume, and the Ovens; and found a beautiful and well-watered country in the vicinity of the coast.

In 1826, Mr. Allan Cunningham, Botanical

Collector to his late Majesty, traversed a considerable portion of the interior to the north of Bathurst, and, with a laudable zeal, devoted his labours to the acquisition of general information, as well as to his more immediate professional pursuits. In 1827, this gentleman again bent his steps towards the northward, and succeeded in gaining the 28th parallel of latitude; and, on a subsequent occasion, having taken his departure from Moreton Bay, he connected his former journey with that settlement, and thus contributed largely to our knowledge of the mountain country between it and the capital. Mr. Cunningham, who, independently of his individual excursions, had not only circumnavigated the Australian Continent with Capt. King, but had formed also one of the party with Mr. Oxley, in the journeys before noticed, had adopted this gentleman's opinion with regard to the swampy and inhospitable character of the distant interior. Its depressed appearance from the high ground on which Mr. Cunningham subsequently moved, tended to confirm this opinion, which was moreover daily gaining strength from the reports of the natives, who became more frequent in their intercourse with the whites, and who reported that there were large waters to the westward, on which the natives had canoes, and in which there were fish of great size.

It became, therefore, a current opinion, that the western interior of New Holland comprehended an extensive basin, of which the ocean of reeds which had proved so formidable to Mr. Oxley, formed most probably the outskirts; and it was generally thought that an expedition proceeding into the interior, would encounter marshes of vast extent, which would be extremely difficult to turn, and no less dangerous to enter.

It remained to be proved, however, whether these conjectures were founded in fact. The chief difficulty lay in the character of the country, and in providing the necessary means to ensure success. Those which were resorted to will be found in the succeeding chapter. Whether they would have been found sufficient and applicable had the interior been wholly under water, is doubtful; and my impression on this point induced me to make more efficient arrangements on the second expedition.

the Karaula, larger than either the Nam
ch obstructed by fallen timber...3 kind
of a friendly disposition with whom t

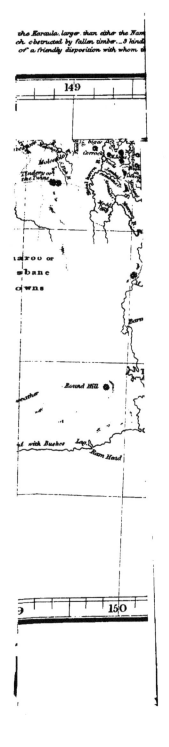

1

EXPEDITION

DOWN THE

BANKS OF THE MACQUARIE RIVER,

In 1828 and 1829.

———

CHAPTER I.

State of the Colony in 1828-29 — Objects of the Expedition — Departure from Sydney — Wellington Valley — Progress down the Macquarie — Arrival at Mount Harris—Stopped by the marshes — Encamp amidst reeds — Excursions down the river — its termination—Appearance of the marshes — Ophthalmic affection of the men — Mr. Hume's successful journey to the northward — Journey across the plain — Second great marsh — Perplexities — Situation of the exploring party — Consequent resolutions.

THE year 1826 was remarkable for the commencement of one of those fearful droughts to which we have reason to believe the climate of New South Wales is periodically subject. It continued during the two following years with unabated severity. The surface of the earth became so parched up that minor vegetation ceased upon it. Culinary herbs were raised with difficulty, and crops failed even in the most favourable situations. Settlers drove their flocks

B

and herds to distant-tracts for pasture and water, neither
remaining for them in the located districts. The interior
suffered equally with the coast, and men, at length, began
to despond under so alarming a visitation. It almost appeared as if the Australian sky were never again to be traversed by a cloud.

But, however severe for the colony the seasons had
proved, or were likely to prove, it was borne in mind at
this critical moment, that the wet and swampy state of
the interior had alone prevented Mr. Oxley from penetrating further into it, in 1818. Each successive report from
Wellington Valley, the most distant settlement to the N.W.,
confirmed the news of the unusually dry state of the lowlands, and of the exhausted appearance of the streams falling into them. It was, consequently, hoped that an expedition, pursuing the line of the Macquarie, would have a
greater chance of success than the late Surveyor General
had ; and that the difficulties he had to contend against
would be found to be greatly diminished, if not altogether
removed. The immediate fitting out of an expedition was
therefore decided upon, for the express purpose of ascertaining the nature and extent of that basin into which the
Macquarie was supposed to fall, and whether any connection
existed between it and the streams falling westerly. As I
had early taken a great interest in the geography of New
South Wales, the Governor was pleased to appoint me to
the command of this expedition.

In the month of September, 1828, I received his Excellency's commands to prepare for my journey; and by the commencement of November, had organized my party, and completed the necessary arrangements. On the 9th of that month, I waited on the Governor, at Paramatta, to receive his definitive instructions. As the establishments at Sydney had been unable to supply me with the necessary number of horses and oxen, instructions had been forwarded to Mr. Maxwell, the superintendent of Wellington Valley, to train a certain number for my use; and I was now directed to push for that settlement without loss of time. I returned to Sydney in the afternoon of the 9th, and on the 10th took leave of my brother officers, to commence a journey of very dubious issue; and, in company with my friend, Staff-surgeon M'Leod, who had obtained permission to accompany me to the limits of the colony, followed my men along the great western road. We moved leisurely over the level country, between the coast and the Nepean River, and availed ourselves of the kind hospitality of those of our friends whose property lay along that line of road, to secure more comfortable places of rest than the inns would have afforded.

We reached Sheane, the residence of Dr. Harris, on the 11th, and were received by him with the characteristic kindness with which friends or strangers are ever welcomed by that gentleman. He had accompanied Mr. Oxley as a volunteer in 1818, and his name was then given to the mount which formed the extreme point to which the main body of the first expedition down the banks of the Macquarie penetrated, in a westerly direction.

The general appearance of the property of Dr. Harris, showed how much perseverance and labour had effected towards its improvement. Many acres of ground bore a promising crop, over which a gloomy forest had once waved. The Doctor's farming establishment was as complete as his husbandry seemed to be prosperous; but he did not appear to be satisfied with the extent of his dwelling, to which he was making considerable additions, although I should have thought it large enough for all ordinary purposes of residence or hospitality. The rewards of successful industry were everywhere visible.

On the 13th, we gained Regent's Ville, the more splendid mansion of Sir John Jamieson, which overlooks the Nepean River, and commands the most beautiful and extensive views of the Blue Mountains. Crossing the ford on the 14th, we overtook the men as they were toiling up the first ascent of those rugged bulwarks, which certainly gave no favourable earnest of the road before us; and, as we could scarcely hope to reach the level country to the westward without the occurrence of some accident, I determined to keep near the drays, that I might be at hand should my presence be required. We gained O'Connel's plains on the 20th November, and arrived at Bathurst on the 22nd, with no other damage than the loss of one of the props supporting the boat which snapped in two as we descended Mount York. On examination, it was found that the boat had also received a slight contusion, but it admitted of easy repair.

I was detained at Bathurst longer than I intended, in consequence of indisposition, and during my stay there experienced many proofs of the kind hospitality of the settlers of that promising district : nor was I ever more impressed with the importance of the service upon which I was employed, or more anxious as to the issue, than while contemplating the rapid advance of agriculture upon its plains, and the formidable bar to its prosperity which I had left behind me, in the dark and gloomy ranges which I had crossed.

On the 27th, Mr. Hamilton Hume, whose experience well qualified him for the task, and who had been associated with me in the expedition, having joined me, we proceeded on our journey, and reached Wellington Valley about the end of the month.

I wished to push into the interior without any delay, or at least, so soon as we should have completed our arrangements and organized the party; but, although Mr. Maxwell had paid every attention to the training of the cattle, he was of opinion that they could not yet be wholly relied upon, and strongly recommended that they should be kept at practice for another week. As we could not have left the settlement under the most favourable circumstances in less than four days, the further delay attendant on this measure was considered immaterial, and it was, accordingly, determined upon. Mr. Hume undertook to superintend the training of the animals, and this left me at leisure to gather such information as would be of use to us in our progress down the river.

In his description of Wellington Valley, Mr. Oxley has not done it more than justice. It is certainly a beautiful and fertile spot, and it was now abundant in pasturage, notwithstanding the unfavourable season that had passed over it.

The settlement stands upon the right bank of the Bell, about two miles above the junction of that stream with the Macquarie. Its whitewashed buildings bore outward testimony to the cleanliness and regularity of the inhabitants; and the respectful conduct of the prisoners under his charge, shewed that Mr. Maxwell had maintained that discipline by which alone he could have secured respect to himself and success to his exertions, at such a distance from the seat of government.

The weather was so exceedingly hot, during our stay, that it was impossible to take exercise at noon; but in the evening, or at an early hour in the morning, we were enabled to make short excursions in the neighbourhood.

Mr. Maxwell informed me that there were three stations below the settlement, the first of which, called Gobawlin, belonging to Mr. Wylde, was not more than five miles from it; the other two, occupied by Mr. Palmer, were at a greater distance, one being nineteen, the other thirty-four miles below the junction of the Bell. He was good enough to send for the stockman (or chief herdsman), in charge of the last, to give me such information of the nature of the country below him, as he could furnish from personal knowledge or from the accounts of the natives.

Mr. Maxwell pointed out to me the spot on which Mr. Oxley's boats had been built, close upon the bank of the Macquarie; and I could not but reflect with some degree of apprehension on the singularly diminished state of the river from what it must then have been to allow a boat to pass down it. Instead of a broad stream and a rapid current, the stream was confined to a narrow space in the centre of the channel, and it ran so feebly amidst frequent shallows that it was often scarcely perceptible. The Bell, also, which Mr. Oxley describes as dashing and rippling along its pebbly bed, had ceased to flow, and consisted merely of a chain of ponds.

On the 3d of Dec. the stockman from below arrived; but the only information we gathered from him was the existence of a lake to the left of the river, about three days' journey below the run of his herds, on the banks of which he assured us, the native companions, a species of stork, stood in rows like companies of soldiers.

He brought up a nest of small paroquets of the most beautiful plumage, as a present to Mr. Maxwell, and affirmed that they were common about his part of the river. The peculiarity of the seasons had also brought a parrot into the valley which had never before visited it. This delicate bird was noticed by Captain Cook upon the coast, and is called *Psittacus Novæ Hollandiæ*, or New Holland Parrot, by Mr. Brown. It had not, however, been subsequently seen until the summer of 1828, when it made its appearance at Wellington Valley in considerable num-

bers, together with a species of merops or mountain bee-
eater.

On the 5th, our preparations being wholly completed,
and the loads arranged, the party was mustered, and was
found to consist of myself and Mr. Hume, two soldiers and
eight prisoners of the crown, two of whom were to return
with dispatches. Our animals numbered two riding, and
seven pack, horses, two draft, and eight pack, bullocks, exclusive of two horses of my own, and two for the men to
be sent back.

The morning of the 7th December, the day upon which
we were to leave the valley, was ushered in by a cloudless
sky, and that heated appearance in the atmosphere which
foretels an oppressively sultry day. I therefore put off the
moment of our departure to the evening, and determined to
proceed no further than Gobawlin. I was the more readily
induced to order this short journey because the animals had
not been practised to their full loads, and I thought they
might have given some trouble at starting with an unusual
weight. They moved off however very quietly, and as if
they had been accustomed to their work by a long course
of training. We took our departure from the settlement
at 3 p. m. and, crossing to the right bank of the Macquarie,
a little above its junction with the Bell, reached Mr.
Wylde's station about half-past 5. Thus we commenced
our journey under circumstances as favorable as could have
been wished. In disengaging ourselves on the following
day from the hills by which Wellington Valley is encompassed on the westward, with a view to approach Mr. Pal-

mer's first station, we kept rather wide of the river, and only occasionally touched on its more projecting angles. The soil at a distance from the stream was by no means so good as that in its immediate vicinity, nor was the timber of the same description. On the rich and picturesque grounds near the river the angophora prevailed with the flooded gum, and the scenery upon its banks was improved by the casuarinæ that overhung them. On the latter, inferior eucalypti and cypresses were mixed together. The country was broken and undulating, and the hills stony, notwithstanding which, they appeared to have an abundance of pasture upon them. Mr. Hume rode with me to the summit of a limestone elevation, from which I thought it probable we might have obtained such a view as would have enabled us to form some idea of the country into which we were about to descend. But in following the river line, the eye wandered over a dark and unbroken forest alone. The ranges from which we were fast receding formed an irregular and beautiful landscape to the southward; and contrasted strongly with the appearance of the country to the N. W., in which direction it was rapidly assuming a level.

We reached Mr. Palmer's at a late hour in the afternoon, in consequence of a delay we experienced in crossing a gully, and encamped upon a high bank immediately opposite to the mouth of Molle's rivulet, which here joins the Macquarie from the southward. The cattle had consumed all the food, and the ground on both sides of the river looked bare and arid.

No doubt, however, the face of the country in ordinary seasons wears a very different appearance. Its general elevation continued high; nor did the Macquarie assume any change of aspect. Mountain debris and rounded pebbles of various kinds formed its bed, which was much encumbered with timber.

We had been unable to persuade any of the natives of Wellington Valley to accompany us as guides, on our leaving that settlement. Even Mr. Maxwell's influence failed; for, notwithstanding the promises of several, when they saw that we were ready to depart, they either feigned sickness or stated that they were afraid of the more distant natives. The fact is, that they were too lazy to wander far from their own district, and too fond of Maxwell's beef to leave it for a precarious bush subsistence. Fortunately we found several natives with Mr. Palmer's stockmen, who readily undertook to conduct us by the nearest route to the cataract, which we considered to be midway between Wellington Valley and Mount Harris. We started under their guidance for Dibilamble, Mr. Palmer's second station, and reached it about half-past 4 p. m. The distance between the two is sixteen miles. The country for some miles differs in no material point from that through which we had already passed. The same rich tracts of soil near the river and the same inferiority in the tracks remote from it. Near Dibilamble, however, the limestone formation terminates, and gives place to barren stony ridges, upon which the cypress callities is of close and stunted growth. The ridges themselves were formed of a coarse kind of freestone in a state of rapid decomposition. The Tabragar (the Erskine of Mr. Oxley) falls into the Macquarie at Dibi-lamble. It had long ceased to flow, being a small moun-tain torrent whose source, if we may judge from the shingly nature of its bed, cannot be very distant. Our descent was considerable during the day; the rapids were frequent in the river, but it underwent no change in its general ap-pearance. Its waters were hard and transparent, and its banks, in many places, extremely lofty; with a red sandy loam and gravel under the alluvial deposits. It generally happened that where the bank was high on the one side, it was low and subject to flood, to a limited extent at least, on the other. Upon these low grounds the blue-gum trees were of lofty growth, but on the upper levels box prevailed.

The views upon the river were really beautiful, and varied at every turn; nor is it possible for any tree to exceed the casuarina in the graceful manner in which it bends over the stream, or clings to some solitary rock in its centre.

It here became necessary for us to cross to the left bank of the river, not only to avoid its numerous windings, and thus to preserve as much as possible the direct line to Mount Harris; but also, because the travelling was much better on the south side. We therefore availed ourselves of a ford opposite to the ground on which the tents had stood; and then pursued our journey, in a south-westerly course, over a country of a description very inferior to that of any we had previously noticed.

Iron-bark and cypresses generally prevailed along our

line of route on a poor and sandy soil, which improved after
we passed Elizabeth Burn, a small creek mentioned by
Mr. Oxley.

We approached the river again early in the day, and pitched our tent on the summit of a sloping bank that overlooked one of its long still reaches. We were protected from the
sun by the angophora trees, which formed a hanging wood
around us, and, with its bright green foliage, gave a cheerfulness to the scene that was altogether unusual. The
opposite side of the river was rather undulated, and the soil
appeared to be of the finest description. The grass, although growing in tufts, afforded abundance of pasture
for the cattle; and, on the whole, this struck me as a
most eligible spot for a station, and I found it occupied as
such on the return of the expedition. We had encamped
about a quarter of a mile from Taylor's Rivulet, which discharges itself into the Macquarie from the N. E., and is
the first stream, upon the right bank, below the Wellington
Valley.

Immediately after receiving it the river sweeps away to
the southward, in consequence of which it became again
necessary for us to cross it. Our guides, who were intelligent lads, led the cattle to a ford, a little below the junction of Taylor's Rivulet, at which we effected a passage
with some difficulty; the opposite bank being very steep, and
we were obliged to force our way up a gully for some eighty
or a hundred yards before we could extricate the team. Pursuing our journey, in a N. W. direction, we soon left the

rich and undulating grounds bordering the river behind us.
A poor, level, and open country, succeeded them. The
soil changed to a light red, sandy loam, on which eucalypti, cypresses, and casuarinæ, were intermixed with
minor shrubs; of which latter, the cherry tree (exocarpus
cupressiformis) was the most prevalent.

At about seven miles from the river we passed some barren freestone ridges, near which Mr. Hume killed the first
kangaroo we had seen. At mid-day we passed a small
creek, at which the cattle were watered; and afterwards
continued our journey through a country similar to that
over which we had already made our way.

As we neared the stream we noticed the acacia pendula
for the first time,— an indication of our approach to the
marshes. The weather still continued extremely hot. Our
journey this day was unusually long, and our cattle suffered so much, and moved so slowly, that it was late when
we struck upon the Macquarie, at a part where its banks
were so high that we had some difficulty in finding a good
watering place.

Being considerably in front of the party, with one of our
guides, when we neared the river, I came suddenly upon
a family of natives. They were much terrified, and finding
that they could not escape, called vehemently to some of
their companions, who were in the distance. By the time
Mr. Hume came up, they had in some measure recovered
their presence of mind, but availed themselves of the first
favourable moment to leave us. I was particular in not

imposing any restraint on these men, in consequence of
which they afterwards mustered sufficient resolution to visit
us in our camp. We now judged that we were about ten
miles from the cataract, and that, according to the accounts of the stockman, we could not be very distant from
the lake he had mentioned.

As I was unwilling to pass any important feature of the
country without enquiry or examination, I requested Mr·
Hume to interrogate the strangers on the subject. They
stated that they belonged to the lake tribe, that the lake
was a short day's journey to the eastward, and that they
would guide us to it if we wished. The matter was accordingly arranged. They left us at dusk, but returned to the
camp at the earliest dawn; when we once more crossed the
river, and, after traversing a very level country for about
nine miles, arrived at our destination. We passed over the
dried beds of lagoons, and through coppices of cypresses
and acacia pendula, or open forest, but did not observe any
of the barren stony ridges so common to the N.E. About
a mile, or a mile and a half, from the lake we examined a
solitary grave that had recently been constructed. It consisted of an oblong mound, with three semicircular seats.
A walk encompassed the whole, from which three others
branched off for a few yards only, into the forest. Several
cypresses, overhanging the grave, were fancifully carved on
the inner side, and on one the shape of a heart was deeply
engraved.

We were sadly disappointed in the appearance of the

lake, which the natives call the Buddah. It is a serpentine sheet of fresh water, of rather more than a mile in length, and from three to four hundred yards in breadth. Its depth was four fathoms; but it seemed as if it were now five or six feet below the ordinary level. No stream either runs into it or flows from it; yet it abounds in fish; from which circumstance I should imagine that it originally owed its supply to the river during some extensive inundation. Notwithstanding that we had crossed some rich tracts of land in our way to it, the neighbourhood of the lake was by no means fertile. The trees around it were in rapid decay, and the little vegetation to be seen appeared to derive but little advantage from its proximity to water.

We had started at early dawn; and the heat had become intolerable long ere the sun had gained the meridian. It was rendered still more oppressive from the want of air in the dense bushes through which we occasionally moved. At 2 p. m. the thermometer stood at 129° of Fahrenheit, in the shade; and at 149° in the sun; the difference being exactly 20°. It is not to be wondered at that the cattle suffered, although the journey was so short. The sun's rays were too powerful even for the natives, who kept as much as possible in the shade. In the evening, when the atmosphere was somewhat cooler, we launched the boat upon the lake, in order to get some wild fowl and fish; but although we were tolerably successful with our guns, we did not take any thing with our hooks.

The natives had, in the course of the afternoon, been

joined by the rest of the tribe, and they now numbered about three and twenty. They were rather distant in their manner, and gazed with apparent astonishment at the scene that was passing before them.

If there had been other proof wanting, of the lamentably parched and exhausted state of the interior, we had on this occasion ample evidence of it, and of the fearful severity of the drought under which the country was suffering. As soon as the sun dipped under the horizon, hundreds of birds came crowding to the border of the lake, to quench the thirst they had been unable to allay in the forest. Some were gasping, others almost too weak to avoid us, and all were indifferent to the reports of our guns.

On leaving the Buddah, eleven only of the natives accompanied us. We reached the river again about noon, on a north-half-east course, where it had a rocky bed, and continued to journey along it, until we reached the cataract, at which we halted. We travelled over soil generally inferior to that which we had seen on the preceding day, but rich in many places. The same kind of timber was observed, but the acacia pendula was more prevalent than any other, although near the river the flooded gum and Australian apple-tree were of beautiful growth.

It had appeared to me that the waters of the Macquarie had been diminishing in volume since our departure from Wellington Valley, and I had a favourable opportunity of judging as to the correctness of this conclusion at the cataract, where its channel, at all times much contracted, was

particularly so on the present occasion. So little force was
there in the current, that I began to entertain doubts how
long it would continue, more especially when I reflected on
the level character of the country we had entered, and the
fact of the Macquarie not receiving any tributary between
this point and the marshes. I was in consequence led to
infer that result, which, though not immediately, eventually took place.

As they were treated with kindness, the natives who accompanied us soon threw off all reserve, and in the afternoon assembled at the pool below the fall to take fish.
They went very systematically to work, with short spears
in their hands that tapered gradually to a point, and sank
at once under water without splash or noise at a given signal from an elderly man. In a short time, one or two rose
with the fish they had transfixed; the others remained
about a minute under water, and then made their appearance near the same rock into the crevices of which they
had driven their prey. Seven fine bream were taken, the
whole of which they insisted on giving to our men, although
I am not aware that any of themselves had broken their
fast that day. They soon, however, procured a quantity of
muscles, with which they sat down very contentedly at a
fire. My barometrical admeasurement gave the cataract
an elevation of 680 feet above the level of the sea; and my
observations placed it in east longitude 148° 3' and in lat.
31° 50' south.

It became an object with us to gain the right bank of

c

the Macquarie as soon as possible; for it was evident that the country to the southward of it was much more swampy than it was to the north : but for some distance below the cataract, we found it impossible to effect our purpose. The rocks composing the bed of the river at the cataract, which are of trapp formation, disappeared at about eight miles below it, when the river immediately assumed another character. Its banks became of equal height, which had not before been the case, and averaged from fifteen to eighteen feet. They were composed entirely of alluvial soil, and were higher than the highest flood-marks. Its waters appeared to be turbid and deep, and its bed was a mixture of sand and clay. The casuarina, which had so often been admired by us, entirely disappeared, and the channel in many places became so narrow as to be completely arched over by gum-trees.

On the 16th, we fell in with a numerous tribe of natives, who joined our train after the very necessary ceremonies of an introduction had passed, and when added to those who still accompanied us, amounted to fifty-three. On this occasion I was riding somewhat in front of the party, when I came upon them. They were very different in appearance from those whom we had surprised at the river; and, from the manner in which I was received, I was led to infer that they had been informed of our arrival, and had purposely assembled to meet us. I was saluted by an old man, who had stationed himself in front of his tribe, and who was their chief. Behind him the young men stood in a line, and behind them the warriors were seated on the ground.

I had a young native with me who had attached himself to our party, and who, from his extreme good nature and superior intelligence, was considered by us as a first-rate kind of fellow. He explained who and what we were, and I was glad to observe that the old chief seemed perfectly reconciled to my presence, although he cast many an anxious glance at the long train of animals that were approaching. The warriors, I remarked, never lifted their eyes from the ground. They were hideously painted with red and yellow ochre, and had their weapons at their sides, while their countenances were fixed, sullen, and determined. In order to overcome this mood, I rode up to them, and, taking a spear from the nearest, gave him my gun to examine; a mark of confidence that was not lost upon them, for they immediately relaxed from their gravity, and as soon as my party arrived, rose up and followed us. That which appeared most to excite their surprise, was the motion of the wheels of the boat carriage. The young native whom I have noticed above, acted as interpreter, and, by his facetious manner, contrived to keep the whole of us in a fit of laughter as we moved along. He had been named Botheri by some stockman.

In consequence of our wish to cross the river, we kept near it, and experienced considerable delay from the frequent marshes that opposed themselves to our progress. In one of these we saw a number of ibises and spoon-

bills; and the natives succeeded in killing two or three
snakes. Our view to the westward was extremely limited;
but to the eastward the country appeared in some places
to expand into plains.

After travelling some miles down the banks of the river,
finding that they still retained their steep character, we
turned back to a place which Mr. Hume had observed, and
at which he thought we might, with some little trouble,
cross to the opposite side. And, however objectionable the
attempt was, we found ourselves obliged to make it. We
descended, therefore, into the channel of the river, and unloaded the animals and boat-carriage. In order to facilitate
the ascent of the right bank, some of the men were directed
to cut steps up it. I was amused to see the natives volun-
tarily assist them; and was surprised when they took up
bags of flour weighing 100lbs. each, and carried them across
the river. We were not long in getting the whole of the
stores over. The boat was then hoisted on the shoulders of
the strongest, and deposited on the top of the opposite
bank; and ropes being afterwards attached to the carriage,
it was soon drawn up to a place of safety. The natives
worked as hard as our own people, and that, too, with a
cheerfulness for which I was altogether unprepared, and
which is certainly foreign to their natural habits. We
pitched our tents as soon as we had effected the passage of
the river; after which, the men went to bathe, and blacks
and whites were mingled promiscuously in the stream. I
did not observe that the former differed in any respect from

the natives who frequent the located districts. They were generally clean limbed and stout, and some of the young men had pleasing intelligent countenances. They lacerate their bodies, inflicting deep wounds to raise the flesh, and extract the front teeth like the Bathurst tribes; and their weapons are precisely the same. They are certainly a merry people, and sit up laughing and talking more than half the night.

During the removal of the stores my barometer was unfortunately broken, and I had often, in the subsequent stages of the journey, occasion to regret the accident. I apprehend that the corks in the instrument, placed to steady the tube, are too distant from each other in most cases; and indeed I fear that barometers as at present constructed, will seldom be carried with safety in overland expeditions.

Nine only of the natives accompanied us on the morning succeeding the day in which we crossed the river. Botheri was, however, at the head of them; and, as we journeyed along, he informed me that he had been promised a wife on his return from acting as our guide, by the chief of the last tribe. The excessive heat of the weather obliged us to shorten our journey, and we encamped about noon in some scrub after having traversed a level country for about eleven miles.

Several considerable plains were noticed to our right, stretching east and west, which were generally rich in point of soil; but we passed through much brushy land during the day. It was lamentable to see the state of vegetation upon the plains from want of moisture. Although the coun-

try had assumed a level character, and was more open than
on the higher branches of the Macquarie, the small free-
stone elevations, backing the alluvial tracts near the river,
still continued upon our right, though much diminished in
height, and at a great distance from the banks. They seemed
to be covered with cypresses and beef-wood, but dwarf-box
and the acacia pendula prevailed along the plains; while
flooded-gum alone occupied the lands in the immediate
neighbourhood of the stream, which was evidently fast
diminishing, both in volume and rapidity; its bed, however,
still continuing to be a mixture of sand and clay.

The cattle found such poor feed around the camp that
they strayed away in search of better during the night. On
such an occasion Botheri and his fraternity would have
been of real service; but he had decamped at an early
hour, and had carried off an axe, a tomahawk, and some
bacon, although I had made him several presents. I was
not at all surprised at this piece of roguery, since cunning is the natural attribute of a savage; but I was
provoked at their running away at a moment when I so
much required their assistance.

Left to ourselves, I found Mr. Hume of the most essential service in tracking the animals, and to his perseverance
we were indebted for their speedy recovery. They had
managed to find tolerable feed near a serpentine sheet of
water, which Mr. Hume thought it would be adviseable to
examine. We directed our course to it as soon as the cattle
were loaded, moving through brush, and found it to be

a very considerable creek that receives a part of the superfluous waters of the Macquarie, and distributes them, most
probably, over the level country to the north. It was much
wider than the river, being from fifty to sixty yards across,
and is resorted to by the natives, who procure muscles from
its bed in great abundance. We were obliged to traverse
its eastern bank to its junction with the river, at which it
fortunately happened to be dry. We had, however, to cut
roads down both its banks before we could cross it; and,
consequently, made but a short day's journey. The soil
passed over was inferior to the generality of soil near the
river, but we encamped on a tongue of land on which both
the flooded-gum and the grass were of luxuriant height.
We found a quantity of a substance like pipe-clay in the
bed of the river, similar to that mentioned by Mr. Oxley.

The heat, which had been excessive at Wellington Valley, increased upon us as we advanced into the interior.
The thermometer was seldom under 114° at noon, and
rose still higher at 2 p. m. We had no dews at night, and
consequently the range of the instrument was trifling in the
twenty-four hours. The country looked bare and scorched,
and the plains over which we journeyed had large fissures
traversing them, so that the earth may literally be said to
have gasped for moisture. The country, which above the
cataract had borne the character of open forest, excepting
on the immediate banks of the river, where its undulations
and openness gave it a park-like appearance, or where the
barren stony ridges prevailed below that point, generally ex-

hibited alternately plain and brush, the soil on both of which was good. On the former, crested pigeons were numerous, several of which were shot. We had likewise procured some of the rose-coloured and grey parrots, mentioned by Mr. Oxley, and a small paroquet of beautiful plumage; but there was less of variety in the feathered race than I expected to find, and most of the other birds we had seen were recognised by me as similar to specimens I had procured from Melville Island, and were, therefore, most probably birds of passage.

As we neared Mount Harris, the Macquarie became more sluggish in its flow, and fell off so much as scarcely to deserve the name of a river. In breadth it averaged from thirty-five to forty-five yards, and in the height of its banks, from fifteen to eighteen. Mr. Hume had succeeded in taking some fish at one of the stock stations; but if I except those speared by the natives, we had since been altogether unsuccessful with the hook, a circumstance which I attribute to the lowness of the river itself.

About thirty miles from the cataract the country declines to the north as a medium point, and again changes somewhat in its general appearance. To the S. and S. W. it appeared level and wooded, while to the N. the plains became more frequent, but smaller, and travelling over them was extremely dangerous, in consequence of the large fissures by which they were traversed. The only trees to be observed were dwarf-box and the acacia pendula, both of stunted growth, although flooded-gum still prevailed upon the river.

THE ROSE COCKATOO.

On the 20th we travelled on a N. W. course, and in the early part of the day passed over tolerably good soil. It was succeeded by a barren scrub, through which we penetrated in the direction of Welcome Rock, a point we had seen from one of the plains and had mistaken for Mount Harris.

On a nearer approach, however, we observed our error, and corrected it by turning more to the left; and we ultimately encamped about a mile to the W. S. W. of the latter eminence. On issuing from the scrub we found ourselves among reeds and coarse water-grass; and, from the appearance of the country, we were led to conclude that we had arrived at a part of the interior more than ordinarily subject to overflow.

As soon as the camp was fixed, Mr. Hume and I rode to Mount Harris, over ground subject to flood and covered for the most part by the polygonum, being too anxious to defer our examination of its neighbourhood even for a few hours.

Nearly ten years had elapsed since Mr. Oxley pitched his tents under the smallest of the two hills into which Mount Harris is broken. There was no difficulty in hitting upon his position. The trenches that had been cut round the tents were still perfect, and the marks of the fire-places distinguishable; while the trees in the neighbourhood had been felled, and round about them the staves of some casks and a few tent-pegs were scattered. Mr. Oxley had selected a place at some distance from the river, in consequence of its then swollen state. I looked upon it from

the same ground, and could not discern the waters in its
channel; so much had they fallen below their ordinary
level.   He saw the river when it was overflowing its banks;
on the present occasion it had scarcely sufficient water to
support a current. On the summit of the greater eminence,
which we ascended, there remained the half-burnt planks of
a boat, some clenched and rusty nails, and an old trunk;
but my search for the bottle Mr. Oxley had left was unsuccessful.

A reflection naturally arose to my mind on examining
these decaying vestiges of a former expedition, whether I
should be more fortunate than the leader of it, and how
far I should be enabled to penetrate beyond the point
which had conquered his perseverance. Only a week before I left Sydney I had followed Mr. Oxley to the tomb.
A man of uncommon quickness, and of great ability, the
task of following up his discoveries was not less enviable
than arduous; but, arrived at that point at which his journey may be said to have terminated and mine only to commence, I knew not how soon I should be obliged, like him,
to retreat from the marshes and exhalations of so depressed
a country. My eye instinctively turned to the North-West,
and the view extended over an apparently endless forest.
I could trace the river line of trees by their superior height;
but saw no appearance of reeds, save the few that grew on
the banks of the stream.

Mount Foster, somewhat higher than Mount Harris, on
the opposite side of the river, alone broke the line of the

horizon to the North N. W. at a distance of five miles.
From that point all round the compass, the low lands spread,
like a dark sea, before me; except where a large plain,
stretching from E. to W., and lying to the S. E. broke their
monotony; and if there was nothing discouraging, there
certainly was nothing cheering, in the prospect.

On our return to the camp, I was vexed to find two of
the men, Henwood and Williams, with increased inflammation of the eyes, of which they had previously been com-
plaining, and I thought it adviseable to bleed the latter.

In consequence of the indisposition of these men, we remained stationary on the 21st, which enabled me to pay a
second visit to Mount Harris. On ascending the smaller
hill, I was surprised to find similar vestiges on its summit
to those I had noticed on the larger one; in addition to
which, the rollers still continued on the side of the hill,
which had been used to get the boat up it.*

Mount Harris is of basaltic formation, but I could not
observe any columnar regularity in it, although large blocks
are exposed above the ground. The rock is extremely hard
and sonorous.

We moved leisurely towards Mount Foster, on the 22d,
and arrived opposite to it a little before sunset. The country between the two is mostly open, or covered only with
the acacia pendula and dwarf-box. The soil, although an

---

* Mr. Oxley had two boats; one of which he dragged to the top of
each of these hills, and left them turned bottom upwards, burying a
bottle under the head of the larger boat, which was conveyed to the
more distant hill.

alluvial deposit, is not of the best; nor was vegetation either fresh or close upon it. As soon as the party stopped, I crossed the river, and lost no time in ascending the hill, being anxious to ascertain if any fresh object was visible from its summit. I thought that from an eminence so much above the level of the surrounding objects, I might obtain a view of the marshes, or of water; but I was wholly disappointed. The view was certainly extensive, but it was otherwise unsatisfactory. Again to the N. W. the lowlands spread in darkness before me; there were some considerable plains beyond the near wood; but the country at the foot of the hill appeared open and promising. Although the river line was lost in the distance, it was as truly pointed out by the fires of the natives, which rose in upright columns into the sky, as if it had been marked by the trees upon its banks.

To the eastward, Arbuthnot's range rose high above the line of the horizon, bearing nearly due East, distant seventy miles. The following sketch of its outlines will convey a better idea of its appearance from Mount Foster than any written description.

I staid on the mount until after sunset, but I could not make out any space that at all resembled the formidable barrier I knew we were so rapidly approaching. I saw nothing to check our advance, and I therefore returned to the camp, to advise with Mr. Hume upon the subject. Not

having been with me on Mount Foster, he took the opportunity to ascend it on the following morning; and on his
return concurred with me in opinion, that there was no
apparent obstacle to our moving onwards. As the men
were considerably better, I had the less hesitation in closing
with the marshes. We left our position, intending to travel
slowly, and to halt early.

The first part of our journey was over rich flats, timbered
sufficiently to afford a shade, on which the grass was luxuriant; but we were obliged to seek more open ground, in
consequence of the frequent stumbling of the cattle.

We issued, at length, upon a plain, the view across which
was as dreary as can be imagined; in many places without
a tree, save a few old stumps left by the natives when they
fired the timber, some of which were still smoking in different parts of it. Observing some lofty trees at the extremity
of the plain, we moved towards them, under an impression
that they indicated the river line. But on this exposed
spot the sun's rays fell with intense power upon us, and the
dust was so minute and penetrating, that I soon regretted
having left the shady banks of the river.

About 2 p. m. we neared the trees for which we had
been making, over ground evidently formed by alluvial de-
position, and were astonished to find that reeds alone were
growing under the trees as far as the eye could penetrate. It
appeared that we were still some distance from the river, and
it was very doubtful how far we might be from water, for
which the men were anxiously calling. I therefore halted,

and sent Fraser into the reeds towards some dead trees, on
which a number of spoonbills were sitting. He found that
there was a small lake in the centre of the reeds, the resort
of numerous wild fowl; but although the men were enabled
to quench their thirst, we found it impossible to water the
animals. We were obliged, therefore, to continue our course
along the edge of the reeds; which in a short time appeared
in large masses in front of us, stretching into a vast plain,
upon our right; and it became evident that the whole neighbourhood was subject to extensive inundation.

I was fearful that the reeds would have checked us; but
there was a passage between the patches, through which we
managed to force our way into a deep bight, and fortunately
gained the river at the bottom of it much sooner than we
expected. We were obliged to clear away a space for the
tents; and thus, although there had been no such appearance from Mount Foster, we found ourselves in less than
seven hours after leaving it, encamped pretty far in that
marsh for which we had so anxiously looked from its summit, and now trusting to circumstances for safety, upon
ground on which, in any ordinary state of the river, it would
have been dangerous to have ventured. Indeed, as it was,
our situation was sufficiently critical, and would not admit
of hesitation on my part.

After the cattle had been turned out, Mr. Hume and I
again mounted our horses, and proceeded to the westward,
with a view to examine the nature of the country before us,
and to ascertain if it was still practicable to move along the

river side. For, although it was evident that we had arrived at what might strictly be called the marshes of the Macquarie, I still thought we might be at some distance from the place where Mr. Oxley terminated his journey.

There was no indication in the river to encourage an idea that it would speedily terminate; nor, although we were on ground subject to extensive inundation, could we be said to have reached the heart of the marshes, as the reeds still continued in detached bodies only. We forced a path through various portions of them, and passed over ground wholly subject to flood, to a distance of about six miles. We then crossed a small rise of ground, sufficiently high to have afforded a retreat, had necessity obliged us to seek for one; and we shortly afterwards descended on the the river, unaltered in its appearance, and rather increased than diminished in size. A vast plain extended to the N.W., the extremity of which we could not discern; though a thick forest formed its northern boundary.

It was evident that this plain had been frequently under water, but it was difficult to judge from the marks on the trees to what height the floods had risen. The soil was an alluvial deposit, superficially sandy; and many shells were scattered over its surface. To the south, the country appeared close and low; nor do I think we could have approached the river from that side, by reason of the huge belts of reeds that appeared to extend as far as the eye could reach.

The approach of night obliged us to return to the camp. On our arrival, we found that the state of Henwood and

Williams would prevent our stirring for a day or two. Not only had they a return of inflammation, but several others of the men complained of a painful irritation of the eyes, which were dreadfully blood-shot and weak. I was in some measure prepared for a relapse in Henwood, as the exposure which he necessarily underwent on the plain was sufficient to produce that effect; but I now became apprehensive that the affection would run through the party.

Considering our situation in its different bearings, it struck me that the men who were to return to Wellington Valley with an account of our proceedings for the Governor's information, had been brought as far as prudence warranted. There was no fear of their going astray, as long as they had the river to guide them; but in the open country which we were to all appearance approaching, or amidst fields of reeds, they might wander from the track, and irrecoverably lose themselves. I determined, therefore, not to risk their safety, but to prepare my dispatches for Sydney, and I hoped most anxiously, that ere they were closed, all symptoms of disease would have terminated.

In the course of the day, however, Spencer, who was to return with Riley to Wellington Valley, became seriously indisposed, and I feared that he was attacked with dysentery. Indeed, I should have attributed his illness to our situation, but I did not notice any unusual moisture in the atmosphere, nor did any fogs rise from the river. I therefore the rather attributed it to exposure and change of diet, and treated him accordingly. To my satisfaction, when I visited the men late in the evening, I found a general improvement in the whole of them. Spencer was considerably relieved, and those of the party who had inflammation of the eyes no longer felt that painful irritation of which they had before complained. I determined, therefore, unless untoward circumstances should prevent it, to send Riley and his companion homewards, and to move the party without loss of time.

We had not seen any natives for many days, but a few passed the camp on the opposite side of the river on the evening of the 25th. They would not, however, come to us; but fled into the interior in great apparent alarm.

On the morning of the 26th, the men were sufficiently recovered to pursue their journey. Riley and Spencer left us at an early hour; and about 7 a. m. we pursued a N.N.W. course along the great plain I have noticed, starting numberless quails, and many wild turkeys, by the way. Leaving that part of the river on which Mr. Hume and I had touched considerably to the left, we made for the point of a wood, projecting from the river line of trees into the plain. The ground under us was an alluvial deposit, and bore all the marks of frequent inundation.

The soil was yielding, blistered, and uneven; and the claws of cray-fish, together with numerous small shells, were every where collected in the hollows made by the subsiding of the waters, between broad belts of reeds and scrubs of polygonum.

On gaining the point of the wood, we found an absolute check put to our further progress. We had been moving directly on the great body of the marsh, and from the wood it spread in boundless extent before us. It was evidently lower than the ground on which we stood; we had, therefore, a complete view over the whole expanse; and there was a dreariness and desolation pervading the scene that strengthened as we gazed upon it. Under existing circumstances, it only remained for us either to skirt the reeds to the northward, or to turn in again upon the river; and as I considered it important to ascertain the direction of the Macquarie at so critical and interesting a point, I thought it better to adopt the latter measure. We, accordingly, made for the river, and pitched our tents, as at the last station, in the midst of reeds.

There were two points, at this time, upon which I was extremely anxious. The first was as to the course of the river; the second, as to the extent of the marshes by which we had been checked, and the practicability of the country to the northward.

In advising with Mr. Hume, I proposed launching the boat, as the surest means of ascertaining the former, and he, on his part, most readily volunteered to examine the marshes, in any direction I should point out. It was, therefore, arranged, that I should take two men, and a week's provision with me in the boat down the river; and that he should proceed with a like number of men on an excursion to the northward.

After having given directions as to the regulations of the camp during our absence, we separated, on the morning of the 26th for the first time, in furtherance of the objects each had in view.

In pulling down the river, I found that its channel was at first extremely tortuous and irregular, but that it held a general N.W. course, and bore much the same appearance as it had done since our descent from Mount Foster.

We had a laborious task in lifting the boat over the trunks of trees that had fallen into the channel of the river or that had been left by the floods, and at length we stove her in upon a sunken log. The injury she received was too serious not to require immediate repair; and we, therefore, patched her up with a tin plate. This accident occasioned some delay, and the morning was consumed without our having made any considerable progress. At length, however, we got into a more open channel.

The river suddenly increased in breadth to thirty-five or forty-five yards, with a depth of from twelve to twenty feet of water. Its banks shelved perpendicularly down, and were almost on a level with the surface of the stream; and the flood mark was not more than two feet high on the reeds by which they were lined. We had hitherto passed under the shade of the flooded gum, which still continued on the immediate banks of the river; but, the farther we advanced, the more did we find these trees in a state of decay, until at length they ceased, or were only rarely met with.

About 2 p. m. I brought up under a solitary tree, in con-

sequence of heavy rain: this was upon the left bank. In
the afternoon, however, we again pushed forward, and soon
lost sight of every other object amidst reeds of great
height. The channel of the river continued as broad and
as deep as ever, but the flood mark did not shew more than
a foot above the banks, which were now almost on a level
with the water; and the current was so sluggish as to be
scarcely perceptible. These general appearances continued
for about three miles, when our course was suddenly, and
most unexpectedly, checked. The channel, which had
promised so well, without any change in its breadth or
depth, ceased altogether; and whilst we were yet lost in
astonishment at so abrupt a termination of it, the boat
grounded. It only remained for us to examine the banks,
which we did with particular attention. Two creeks were
then discovered, so small as scarcely to deserve the name,
and which would, under ordinary circumstances, have
been overlooked. The one branched off to the north — the
other to the west. We were obliged to get out of the boat
to push up the former, the leeches sticking in numbers to
our legs. The creek continued for about thirty yards,
when it was terminated; and, in order fully to satisfy myself of the fact, I walked round the head of it by pushing
through the reeds. Night coming on, we returned to the
tree at which we had stopped during the rain, and slept
under it. The men cut away the reeds, or we should not
have had room to move. At 2 a. m. it commenced rain-
ing, with a heavy storm of thunder and lightning; the

boat was consequently hauled ashore, and turned over to afford us a temporary shelter. The lightning was extremely vivid, and frequently played upon the ground, near the firelocks, for more than a quarter of a minute at a time.

It is singular, that Mr. Oxley should, under similar circumstances, have experienced an equally stormy night, and most probably within a few yards of the place on which I had posted myself. Notwithstanding that the elements were raging around me, as if to warn me of the danger of my situation, my mind turned solely on the singular failure of the river. I could not but encourage hopes that this second channel that remained to be explored would lead us into an open space again; and as soon as the morning dawned we pursued our way to it. In passing some dead trees upon the right bank, I stopped to ascend one, that, from an elevation, I might survey the marsh, but I found it impossible to trace the river through it. The country to the westward was covered with reeds, apparently to the distance of seven miles; to the N.W. to a still greater distance; and to the north they bounded the horizon.

The whole expanse was level and unbroken, but here and there the reeds were higher and darker than at other places, as if they grew near constant moisture; but I could see no appearance of water in any body, or of high lands beyond the distant forest.

As soon as we arrived at the end of the main channel, we again got out of the boat, and in pushing up the smaller one, soon found ourselves under a dark arch of reeds.

It did not, however, continue more than twenty yards when it ceased, and I walked round the head of it as I had done round that of the other. We then examined the space between the creeks, where the bank receives the force of the current, which I did not doubt had formed them by the separation of its eddies. Observing water among the reeds, I pushed through them with infinite labour to a considerable distance. The soil proved to be a stiff clay; the reeds were closely embodied, and from ten to twelve feet high; the waters were in some places ankle deep, and in others scarcely covered the surface. They were flowing in different points, with greater speed than those of the river, which at once convinced me that they were not permanent, but must have lodged in the night during which so much rain had fallen. They ultimately appeared to flow to the northward, but I found it impossible to follow them, and it was not without difficulty that, after having wandered about at every point of the compass, I aaain reached the boat.

The care with which I had noted every change that took place in the Macquarie, from Wellington Valley downwards, enabled me, in some measure, to account for its present features. I was led to conclude that the waters of the river being so small in body, excepting in times of flood, and flowing for so many miles through a level country without receiving any tributary to support their first impulse, became too sluggish, long ere they reached the marshes, to cleave through so formidable a barrier; and consequently spread over the surrounding country—whether again to take up the character of a river, we had still to determine. Unless, however, a decline of country should favour its assuming its original shape, it was evident that the Macquarie would not be found to exist beyond this marsh, of the nature and extent of which we were still ignorant. The loss of my barometer was at this time severely felt by me, since I could only guess at our probable height above the ocean; and I found that my only course was to endeavour to force my way to the northward, to ascertain, if I could, from the bottom of the marshes; then penetrate in a westerly direction beyond them, in order to commence my survey of the S. W. interior. I was aware of Mr. Hume's perseverance, and determined, therefore, to wait the result of his report ere I again moved the camp, to which we returned late in the afternoon of the second day of our departure. We found it unsufferably hot and suffocating in the reeds, and were tormented by myriads of mosquitoes, but the waters were perfectly sweet to the taste, nor did the slightest smell, as of stagnation, proceed from them. I may add that the birds, whose sanctuary we had invaded, as the bittern and various tribes of the galinule, together with the frogs, made incessant noises around us. There were, however, but few waterfowl on the river; which was an additional proof to me that we were not near any very extensive lake,

Mr. Hume had returned before me to the camp, and had succeeded in finding a serpentine sheet of water, about twelve miles to the northward; which he did not doubt to be the channel of the river. He had pushed on after this

success, in the hope of gaining a further knowledge of the
country; but another still more extensive marsh checked
him, and obliged him to retrace his steps.   He was no less
surprised at the account I gave of the termination of the
river, than I was at its so speedily re-forming, and it was
determined to lose no time in the further examination of so
singular a region.

On the morning of the 28th therefore we broke up the
camp, and proceeded to the northward, under Mr. Hume's
guidance, moving over ground wholly subject to flood,
and extensively covered with reeds; the great body of
the marsh lying upon our left.   After passing the angle
of a wood, upon our right, from which Mount Foster
was distant about fourteen miles, we got upon a small
plain, on which there was a new species of tortuous box.
This plain was clear of reeds, and the soil upon it was very
rich.   Crossing in a westerly direction we arrived at the
channel found by Mr. Hume, who must naturally have concluded that it was a continuation of the river.   The boat
was immediately prepared, and I went up it in order to
ascertain the nature of its formation.   For two miles it preserved a pretty general width of from twenty to thirty yards;
but at that distance began to narrow, and at length it became quite shallow and covered with weeds.   We were
ultimately obliged to abandon the boat, and to walk along
a native path.   The country to the westward was more open
than I had expected.   About a quarter of a mile from where
we had left the boat, the channel separated into two

branches; to which I perceived it owed its formation, coming, as they evidently did, direct from the heart of the marsh. The wood through which I had entered it on the first occasion bore south of me, to which one of the branches inclined; as the other did to the S. W. An almost imperceptible rise of ground was before me, which, by giving an impetus to the waters of the marsh, accounted to me for the formation of the main channel. It was too late, on my return to the camp, to prosecute any further examination of it downwards; but in the morning, Mr. Hume accompanied me in the boat, to ascertain to what point it led; and we found that at about a mile it began to diminish in breadth, until at length it was completely lost in a second expanse of reeds. We passed a singular scaffolding erected by the natives, on the side of the channel, to take fish; and also found a weir at the termination of it for the like purpose, so that it was evident the natives occasionally ventured into the marshes.

There was a small wood to our left which Mr. Hume endeavoured to gain, but he failed in the attempt. He did, however, reach a tree that was sufficiently high to give him a full view of the marsh, which appeared to extend in every direction, but more particularly to the north, for many miles. We were, however, at fault, and I really felt at a loss what step to take. I should have been led to believe, from the extreme flatness of the country, that the Macquarie would never assume its natural shape, but from the direction of the marshes I could not but indulge a hope that it

would meet the Castlereagh, and that their united waters
might form a stream of some importance.   Under this impression I determined on again sending Mr. Hume to the
N. E. in order to ascertain the nature of the country in that
direction.

The weather was excessively hot, and as my men were
but slowly recovering, I was anxious while those who were
in health continued active, to give the others a few days of
rest.   I proposed, therefore, to cross the river, and to make
an excursion into the interior, during the probable time of
Mr. Hume's absence ; since · if, as I imagined, the Macquarie had taken a permanent northerly course, I should
not have an opportunity of examining the distant western
country.   Mr. Hume's experience rendered it unnecessary
for me to give him other than general directions.

On the last day of the year we left the camp, each accompanied by two men.   I had the evening previously ordered the horses I intended taking with me across the channel, and at an early hour of the morning I followed them.
Getting on a plain, immediately after I had disengaged
myself from the reeds on the opposite side of the river,
which was full of holes and exceedingly treacherous for the
animals, I pushed on for a part of the wood Mr. Hume had
endeavoured to gain from the boat, with the intention of
keeping near the marsh.   On entering it, I found myself
in a thick brush of eucalypti, casuarinæ and minor trees; the
soil under them being mixed with sand.   I kept a N. N. W.
course through it, and at the distance of three miles from

its commencement, ascended a tree, to ascertain if I was near the marshes; when I found that I was fast receding from them. I concluded, therefore, that my conjecture as to their direction was right, and altered my course to N.W., a direction in which I had observed a dense smoke arising, which I supposed had been made by some natives near water. At the termination of the brush I crossed a barren sandy plain, and from it saw the smoke ascending at a few miles' distance from me. Passing through a wood, at the extremity of the plain, I found myself at the out-skirts of an open space of great extent, almost wholly en-veloped in flames. The fire was running with incredible rapidity through the rhagodia shrubs with which it was covered. Passing quickly over it, I continued my journey to the N.W. over barren plains of red sandy loam of even surface, and bushes of cypresses skirted by acacia pendula. It was not until after sunset that we struck upon a creek, in which the water was excellent; and we halted on its banks for the night, calculating our distance at twenty-nine miles from the camp. The creek was of considerable size, leading northerly. Several huts were observed by us, and from the heaps of muscle-shells that were scattered about, there could be no doubt of its being much frequented by the natives. The grass being fairly burnt up, our animals found but little to eat, but they had a tolerable journey, and did not at-tempt to wander in search of better food. I shot a snipe near the creek, much resembling the painted snipe of India; but I had not the means with me of preserving it.

Continuing our journey on the following morning, we at first kept on the banks of the creek, and at about a quarter of a mile from where we had slept, came upon a numerous tribe of natives. A young girl sitting by the fire was the first to observe us as we were slowly approaching her. She was so excessively alarmed, that she had not the power to run away; but threw herself on the ground and screamed violently. We now observed a number of huts, out of which the natives issued, little dreaming of the spectacle they were to behold. But the moment they saw us, they started back; their huts were in a moment in flames, and each with a fire-brand ran to and fro with hideous yells, thrusting them into every bush they passed. I walked my horse quietly towards an old man who stood more forward than the rest, as if he intended to devote himself for the preservation of his tribe. I had intended speaking to him, but on a nearer approach I remarked that he trembled so violently that it was impossible to expect that I could obtain any information from him, and as I had not time for explanations, I left him to form his own conjectures as to what we were, and continued to move towards a thick brush, into which they did not venture to follow us.

After a ride of about eighteen miles, through a country of alternate plain and brush, we struck upon a second creek leading like the first to the northward. The water in it was very bitter and muddy, and it was much inferior in appearance to that at which we had slept. After stopping for half-an-hour upon its banks, to rest our animals, we again pushed forward. We had not as yet risen any perceptible height above the level of the marshes, but had left the country subject to overflow for a considerable space behind us. The brushes through which we had passed were too sandy to retain water long, but the plains were of such an even surface, that they could not but continue wet for a considerable period after any fall of rain. They were covered with salsolaceous plants, without a blade of grass; and their soil was generally a red sandy loam. There were occasional patches that appeared moist, in which the calystemma was abundant, and these patches must, I should imagine, form quagmires in the wet season.

On leaving the last-mentioned creek, we found a gently rising country before us; and about three or four miles from it we crossed some stony ridges, covered with a new species of acacia so thickly as to prevent our obtaining any view from them. As the sun declined, we got into open forest ground; and travelled forwards in momentary expectation, from appearances, of coming in sight of water; but we were obliged to pull up at sunset on the outskirts of a larger plain without having our expectation realized. The day had been extremely warm, and our animals were as thirsty as ourselves. Hope never forsakes the human breast; and thence it was that, after we had secured the horses, we began to wander round our lonely bivouac. It was almost dark, when one of my men came to inform me that he had found a small puddle of water, to which he had been led by a pigeon.

It was, indeed, small enough, probably the remains of a passing shower; it was, however, sufficient for our necessities, and I thanked Providence for its bounty to us. We were now about sixty miles from the Macquarie, in a N. W. by W. direction, and the country had proved so extremely discouraging, that I intimated to my men my intention of retracing my steps, should I not discover any change in it before noon on the morrow. A dense brush of acacia succeeded to the plain on which we had slept, which we entered, and shortly afterwards found ourselves in an open space, of oblong shape, at the extremity of which there was a shallow lake. The brush completely encircled it, and a few huts were upon its banks. About 10 p: m. we got into an open forest track of better appearance than any over which we had recently travelled.

There was a visible change in the country, and the soil, although red, was extremely rich and free from sand. A short time afterwards we rose to the summit of a round hill, from which we obtained an extensive view on most points of the compass. We had imperceptibly risen considerably above the general level of the interior.

Beneath us, to the westward, I observed a broad and thinly wooded valley; and W. by S., distant apparently about twenty miles, an isolated mountain, whose sides seemed almost perpendicular, broke the otherwise even line of the horizon; but the country in every other direction looked as if it was darkly wooded. Anticipating that I should find a stream in the valley, I did not for a moment hesitate in

striking down into it. Disappointed, however, in this expectation, I continued onwards to the mountain, which I
reached just before the sun set. Indeed, he was barely visible when I gained its summit; but my eyes, from exposure to his glare, became so weak, my face was so blistered,
and my lips cracked in so many places, that I was unable
to look towards the west, and was actually obliged to sit
down behind a rock until he had set.

Perhaps no time is so favourable for a view along the
horizon as the sunset hour; and here, at an elevation of
from five to six hundred feet above the plain, the visible
line of it could not have been less than from thirty-five to
forty-five miles. The hill upon which I stood was broken
into two points; the one was a bold rocky elevation; the
other had its rear face also perpendicular, but gradually declined to the north, and at a distance of from four to five
miles was lost in an extensive and open plain in that direction. In the S. E. quarter, two wooded hills were visible,
which before had appeared to be nothing more than swells
in the general level of the country. A small hill, similar to
the above, bore N. E. by compass; and again, to the west,
a more considerable mountain than that I had ascended,
and evidently much higher, reflected the last beams of the
sun as he sunk behind them. I looked, however, in vain
for water. I could not trace either the windings of a stream,
or the course of a mountain torrent; and, as we had passed
a swamp about a mile from the hill, we descended to it for
the night, during which we were grievously tormented by
the mosquitoes.

I had no inducement to proceed further into the interior.
I had been sufficiently disappointed in the termination of
this excursion, and the track before me was still less invit-
ing. Nothing but a dense forest, and a level country, existed between me and the distant hill. I had learnt, by
experience, that it was impossible to form any opinion of
the probable features of so singular a region as that in which
I was wandering, from previous appearances, or to expect
the same result, as in other countries, from similar causes.
In a geographical point of view, my journey had been more
successful, and had enabled me to put to rest for ever a
question of much previous doubt. Of whatever extent the
marshes of the Macquarie might be, it was evident they
were not connected with those of the Lachlan. I had
gained a knowledge of more than 100 miles of the western
interior, and had ascertained that no sea, indeed that little
water, existed on its surface ; and that, although it is generally flat, it still has elevations of considerable magnitude
upon it.

Although I had passed over much barren ground, I had
likewise noticed soil that was far from poor, and the vegetation upon which in ordinary seasons would, I am convinced, have borne a very different aspect.

Yet, upon the whole, the space I traversed is unlikely to
become the haunt of civilized man, or will only become so
in isolated spots, as a chain of connection to a more fertile
country ; if such a country exist to the westward.

The hill which thus became the extreme of my journey,

is of sandstone formation, and is bold and precipitous. Its summit is level and lightly timbered. As a tribute of respect to the late Surveyor-General, I called it Oxley's Table Land, and I named the distant hills D'Urban's Group, after Sir Benjamin D'Urban, in compliance with a previous request of my friend Lieut. De la Condamine, that I would so name any prominent feature of the interior that I might happen to come upon.

In returning to the camp, I made a circuit to the N. E., and reached the Macquarie late on the evening of the 5th of January; having been absent six days, during which we could not have ridden less than 200 miles. Yet the horses were not so fatigued as it was natural to expect they would have been.

My servant informed me that a party of natives had visited the camp on the 3d, but that they retired precipitately on seeing the animals. I regretted to find the men but little better than when I left them. Several still complained of a painful irritation of the eyes, and of great weakness of sight. Attributing their continued indisposition in some measure to our situation, I was anxious to have moved from it; but as Mr. Hume was still absent, I could not decide upon the measure. He made his appearance, however, on the 6th, having ridden the greater part of the day through rain, which commenced to fall in the morning. Soon after his arrival, Dawber, my overseer of animals, who had accompanied him, was taken suddenly ill. During the night he became much worse, with shiverings and spasms, and on the

E

following morning he was extremely weak and feverish. To
add to my anxiety, Mr. Hume also complained of indisposition. His state of health made me the more anxious to
quit a position which I fancied unwholesome, and in which,
if there was no apparent, there was certainly some secret,
exciting cause; and as Mr. Hume reported having crossed
a chain of ponds about four miles to the eastward, and out
of the immediate precincts of the marshes, I ordered the
tents to be struck, and placing Dawber on my horse, we all
moved quietly over to them.

The result of Mr. Hume's journey perplexed me exceedingly. He stated, that on setting out from the Macquarie
his intention was to have proceeded to the N. E., to ascertain how far the reeds existed in that direction, and, if at
all practicable, to reach the Castlereagh; but in case of
failure, to regain the Macquarie by a westerly course. At
first he travelled nearly four miles east, to clear the marshes,
when he came on the chain of ponds to which we had removed.

He travelled over good soil for two miles after crossing
this chain of ponds, but afterwards got on a red sandy loam,
and found it difficult to proceed, by reason of the thickness
of the brush, and the swampy state of the ground in consequence of the late rain.

The timber in the brushes was of various kinds, and he
saw numerous kangaroos and emus. On issuing from this
brush, he crossed a creek, leading northerly, the banks of
which were from ten to twelve feet high. Whatever the

body of water usually in it is, it now only afforded a few shallow puddles. Mr. Hume travelled through brushes until he came upon a third creek, similar to the one he had left behind him, at which he halted for the night. The water in it was bad, and the feed for the animals extremely poor. The brush lined the creek thickly, and consisted chiefly of acacia pendula and box. The country preserved an uniform level, nor did Mr. Hume, from the highest trees, observe any break on the horizon.

On the 2d of January, Mr. Hume kept more northerly, being unable to penetrate the brushes he encountered. At two miles he crossed a creek leading to the N.W., between which and the place at which he had slept, he passed a native burial ground, containing eight graves. The earth was piled up in a conical shape, but the trees were not carved over as he had seen them in most other places.

The country became more open after he had passed the last mentioned creek, which he again struck upon at the distance of eight miles, and as it was then leading to the N.N.E. he followed it down for eighteen or twenty miles, and crossed it frequently during the day. The creek was dry in most places, and where he stopped for the night the water was bad, and the cattle feed indifferent.

Mr. Hume saw many huts, but none of them had been recently occupied, although large quantities of muscle-shells were scattered about. He computed that he had travelled about thirty miles, in a N.N.W. direction, and the whole of the land he passed over was, generally speaking, bad, nor did it appear to be subject to over-flow.

On the 3d, Mr. Hume proceeded down the creek on which he had slept, on a northern course, under an impression that it would have joined the Castlereagh, but it took a N.W. direction after he had ridden about four miles, and then turned again to the eastward of north. In conse-quence of this, he left it, and proceeded to the westward, being of opinion that the river just mentioned must have taken a more northerly course than Mr. Oxley supposed it to have done.

A short time after Mr. Hume turned towards the Mac-quarie, the country assumed a more pleasing appearance. He soon cleared the brushes, and at two miles came upon a chain of ponds, again running northerly in times of flood. Shortly after crossing these, he found himself on an exten-sive plain, apparently subject to overflow. The timber on it was chiefly of the blue-gum kind, and the ground was covered with shells. He then thought he was approach-ing the Macquarie, and proceeded due west across the flat for about two miles. At the extremity of it there was a hollow, which he searched in vain for water. Ascending about thirty feet, he entered a thick brush of box and acacia pendula, which continued for fourteen miles, when it terminated abruptly, and extensive plains of good soil commenced, stretching from N. to S. as far as the eye could reach, on which there were many kangaroos. Con-tinuing to journey over them, he reached a creek at five p. m.

on which the wild fowl were numerous, running nearly north and south, and he rested on its banks for the night. The timber consisted both of blue and rough gum, and the soil was a light earth.

Mr. Hume expected in the course of the day to have reached the Macquarie, but on arriving at the creek, he began to doubt whether it any longer existed, or whether it had not taken a more westerly direction. On the following morning, therefore, he crossed the creek, and travelled W. S. W., for about two miles over good plains; then through light brushes of swamp-oak, cypress, box, and acacia pendula, for about twelve miles, to another creek leading northerly. He shortly afterwards ascended a range of hills stretching W.N.W. to which he gave the name of New Year's Range. From these hills, he had an extensive view, although not upon the highest part, but the only break he could see in the horizon was caused by some hills bearing by compass W. by S. distant about twenty-five miles. There was, however, an appearance as of high land to the northward, although Mr. Hume thought it might have been an atmospheric deception. From the range he looked in vain for the Macquarie, or other waters, and, as his provisions were nearly consumed, he was obliged to give up all further pursuit, and to retrace his steps. He fell in with two parties of natives, which, taken collectively, amounted to thirty-five in number, but had no communication with them.

It was evident, from the above account, that supposing a

line to have been drawn from the camp northerly, Mr.
Hume must have travelled considerably to the westward
of it, and as I had run on a N. W. course from the
marshes, it necessarily followed that our lines of route
must have intersected each other, or that want of extension
could alone have prevented them from having done so; but
that, under any circumstances, they could not have been very
far apart. This was too important a point to be left undecided, as upon it the question of the Macquarie's termination
seemed to depend.

Both Mr. Hume and myself were of opinion, that a medium
course would be the most satisfactory for us to pursue,
to decide this point; and it appeared that we could not do
better than, by availing ourselves of the creek on which we
were, and skirting the reeds, to take the first opportunity
of dashing through them in a westerly direction.

I entertained great doubts as to the longer existence of
the river, and as I foresaw that, in the event of its having
terminated we should strike at once into the heart of the
interior, I became anxious for the arrival of supplies at
Mount Harris; and although I could hardly expect that
they had yet reached it, I determined to proceed thither.
Mr. Hume was too unwell for me to think of imposing
additional fatigue upon him; I left him, therefore, to conduct the party, by easy stages, to the northward, until
such time as I should overtake them. Even in one day there
was a visible improvement in the men, and Dawber's attack
seemed to be rather the effects of cold than of any thing

else. A death, however, under our circumstances, would have been so truly deplorable an event, that the least illness was sufficient to create alarm.

I can hardly say that I was disappointed on my arrival at Mount Harris, to find its neighbourhood silent and deserted. I remained, however, under it for the greater part of the next day, and, prior to leaving it, placed a sheet of paper with written instructions against a tree, though almost without a hope that it would remain untouched.

A little after sun-set we reached the first small marsh, at which we slept; and on the following morning I crossed the plains of the Macquarie, and joined the party at about fifteen miles from the creek at which I had left it. I found it in a condition that was as unlooked for by Mr. Hume as it was unexpected by me, and really in a most perplexing situation.

On the day I left him, Mr. Hume only advanced about two miles, in consequence of some derangement in the loads. Having crossed the creek, he, the next morning, proceeded down its right bank, until it entered the marshes and was lost. He then continued to move on the outskirts of the latter, and having performed a journey of about eight miles, was anxious to have stopped, but there was no water at hand. The men, however, were so fatigued, in consequence of previous illness, that he felt it necessary to halt after travelling about eleven miles.

No water could be procured even here, notwithstanding that Mr. Hume, who was quite unfit for great exertion, under-

went considerable bodily fatigue in his anxiety to find some.
He was, therefore, obliged to move early on the following
morning, but neither men nor animals were in a condition
to travel; and he had scarcely made three miles' progress,
when he stopped and endeavoured to obtain a supply of
water by digging pits among the reeds. From these he had
drawn sufficient for the wants of the people when I arrived. Some rain had fallen on the 6th and 7th of the
month, or it is more than probable the expedient to which
he resorted would have failed of success. Mr. Hume, I
was sorry to observe, looked very unwell; but nothing could
prevent him from further endeavours to extricate the party
from its present embarrassment.

As soon as I had taken a little refreshment, therefore, I
mounted a fresh horse; and he accompanied me across a
small plain, immediately in front of the camp, which was
subject to overflow and covered with polygonum, having a
considerable extent of reeds to its right.

From the plain we entered a wood of blue-gum, in which
reeds, grass, and brush formed a thick coppice. We at
length passed into an open space, surrounded on every side
by weeds in dense bodies. The great marsh bore south of
us, and was clear and open, but behind us the blue-gum
trees formed a thick wood above the weeds.

About two hundred yards from the outskirts of the marsh
there was a line of saplings that had perished, and round
about them a number of the tern tribe (sea swallow) were
flying, one of which Mr. Hume had followed a consider-

able way into the reeds the evening before, in the hope that it would have led him to water. The circumstance of their being in such numbers led us to penetrate towards them, when we found a serpentine sheet of water of some length, over which they were playing. We had scarcely time to examine it before night closed in upon us, and it was after nine when we returned to the tents.

From the general appearance of the country to the northward, and from the circumstance of our having got to the bottom of the great marsh, which but a few days before had threatened to be so formidable, I thought it probable that the reeds would not again prove so extensive as they had been, and I determined, if I could do so, to push through them in a westerly direction from our position.

The pits yielded us so abundant a supply during the night, that in the morning we found it unnecessary to take the animals to water at the channel we had succeeded in finding the evening before; but pursuing a westerly course we passed it, and struck deep into the reeds. At mid-day we were hemmed in by them on every side, and had crossed over numerous channels, by means of which the waters of the marshes are equally and generally distributed over the space subject to their influence. Coming to a second sheet of water, narrower, but longer, as well as we could judge, than the first, we stopped to dine at it; and, while the men were resting themselves, Mr. Hume rode with me in a westerly direction, to ascertain what obstacles we still had to contend with. Forcing our way through bodies of reeds, we at length got on a plain, stretching from S. E. to N.W., bounded on the right by a wood of blue-gum, under which the reeds still extended, and on the left by a wood in which they did not appear to exist. Certain that there was no serious obstacle in our way, we returned to the men; and as soon as they had finished their meal, led them over the plain in a N. W. by W. direction. It was covered with shells, and was full of holes from the effects of flood.

As we were journeying over it, I requested Mr. Hume to ride into the wood upon our left, to ascertain if it concealed any channel. On his return he informed me that he descended from the plain into a hollow, the bottom of which was covered with small shells and bulrushes. He observed a new species of eucalypti, on the trunks of which the water-mark was three feet high. After crossing this hollow, which was about a quarter of a mile in breadth, he gained an open forest of box, having good grass under it; and, judging from the appearance of the country that no other channel could exist beyond him, and that he had ascertained sufficient for the object I had in view, he turned back to the plain. We stopped for the night under a wood of box, where the grass, which had been burnt down, was then springing up most beautifully green, and was relished exceedingly by the animals.

It was in consequence of our not having crossed any channel, while penetrating through the reeds, that could

by any possible exaggeration have been laid down as the
bed of the river, that I detached Mr. Hume; and the account he brought me at once confirmed my opinion in regard to the Macquarie, and I thenceforth gave up every
hope of ever seeing it in its characteristic shape again.

Independently however of all circumstantial evidence, it
was clear that the river had not re-formed at a distance of
twenty-five miles to the north of us, since Mr. Hume had
gone to the westward of that point, at about the same distance on his late journey, without having observed the
least appearance of reeds or of a river. He had, indeed,
noticed a hollow, which occasionally contained water, but
he saw nothing like the bed of a permanent stream. I
became convinced, also, from observation of the country
through which we had passed, that the sources of the Macquarie could not be of such magnitude as to give a constant
flow to it as a river, and at the same time to supply with
water the vast concavity into which it falls. In very
heavy rains only could the marshes and adjacent lands be
laid wholly under water, since the evaporation alone would
be equal to the supply.

The great plains stretching for so many miles to the
westward of Mount Harris, even where they were clear of
reeds, were covered with shells and the claws of cray-fish,
and their soil, although an alluvial deposit, was superficially sandy. They bore the appearance not only of frequent inundation, but of the floods having eventually
subsided upon them. This was particularly observable at

the bottom of the marshes. We did not find any accumulation of rubbish to indicate a rush of water to any one point; but numerous minor channels existed to distribute the floods equally and generally over every part of the area subject to them, and the marks of inundation and subsidence were everywhere the same. The plain we had last crossed, was, in like manner, covered with shells, so that we could not yet be said to be out of the influence of the marshes; besides which we had not crossed the hollow noticed by Mr. Hume, which it was clear we should do, sooner or later.

To have remained in our position would have been impossible, as there was no water either for ourselves or the animals; to have descended into the reeds again, for the purpose of carrying on a minute survey, would, under existing circumstances, have been imprudent. Our provisions were running short, and if a knowledge of the distant interior was to be gained, we had no time to lose. It was determined, therefore, to defer our further examination of the marshes to the period of our return; and to pursue such a course as would soonest and most effectually enable us to determine the character of the western interior.

CHAPTER II.

WE left our position at the head of the plain early on
the 13th of January, and, ere the sun dipped, had entered a
very different country from that in which we had been
labouring for the last three weeks. We had, as yet, passed
over little other than an alluvial soil, but found that it
changed to a red loam in the brushes immediately backing
the camp.   An open forest track succeeded this, over
which the vegetation had an unusual freshness, indicating
that the waters had not long subsided from its surface.
We shortly afterwards crossed a hollow, similar to that Mr.
Hume had described, in which bulrushes had taken the
place of reeds. Flooded-gum trees, of large size, were also
growing in it, but on either side box alone prevailed, under
whicht he forest grass grew to a considerable height.   We
crossed the hollow two or three times, and as often remarked the line of separation between those trees.   The

last time we crossed it the country rose a few feet, and we journeyed for the remainder of the day, at one time over good plains, at another through brushes, until we found water and feed, at which we stopped for the night, after having travelling about thirteen miles on a W. by N. course. The mosquitoes were so extremely troublesome at this place that we called it Mosquito Brush. At this time my men were improving rapidly, and Mr. Hume complained less, and looked better. I hoped, therefore, that our progress would be rapid into the interior.

On the 14th we took up a westerly course, and in the first instance traversed a plain of great extent; the soil of which was for the most part a red sandy loam, but having patches of light earth upon it. The former was covered with plants of the chenopedia kind; the latter had evidently been quagmires, and bore even then the appearance of moisture. At about seven miles from Mosquito Brush we struck upon a creek of excellent water, upon which the wild fowl were numerous. Some natives was seen, but they were only women, and seemed so alarmed that I purposely avoided them. As the creek was leading northerly, we traced it down on that course for about seven miles, and then halted upon its banks, which were composed of a light tenacious earth. Brushes of casuarina existed near it, but a tortuous box was the prevailing tree, which, excepting for the knees of small vessels, could not have been applied to any use, while the flooded-gum had entirely disappeared. Some ducks were shot in the afternoon, which proved a great treat, as we had been living for some time on salt provisions. Our animals fared worse than ourselves, as the bed of the creek was occupied by coarse rushes, and but little vegetation was elsewhere to be seen. I here killed a beautiful snake, of about four feet in length, and of a bright yellow colour: I had not, however, the means of preserving it. Fraser collected numerous botanical specimens, and among them two kinds of caparis. Indeed a great alteration had taken place in the minor shrubs, and few of those now prevalent had been observed to the eastward of the marshes.

From the creek, which both I and Mr. Hume must have crossed on our respective journeys, we held a westerly course for about fifteen miles, through a country of alternate plain and brush, the latter predominating, and in its general character differing but little from that we had traversed the day previous.

The acacia pendula still continued to exist on the plains, backed by dark rows of cypresses.* In the brushes, box and casuarina, † with several other kinds of eucalypti, prevailed; but none of them were sufficiently large to be of use. The plains were so extremely level that a meridian altitude could have been taken without any material error; and I doubt much whether it would have been possible to have traversed them had the season been wet.

As we were travelling through a forest we surprised a hunting party of natives. Mr. Hume and I were considerably in front of our party at the time, and he only had his

* Cupressus callitris.　　　† Casuarina tortuosa.

gun with him. We had been moving along so quietly that
we were not for some time observed by them. Three were
seated on the ground, under a tree, and two others were
busily employed on one of the lower branches cutting out
honey. As soon as they saw us, four of them ran away;
but the fifth, who wore a cap of emu feathers, stood for a
moment looking at us, and then very deliberately dropped
out of the tree to the ground. I then advanced towards
him, but before I got round a bush that intervened, he had
darted away. I was fearful that he was gone to collect his
tribe, and, under this impression, rode quickly back for my
gun to support Mr. Hume. On my arrival I found the
native was before me. He stood about twenty paces from
Mr. Hume, who was endeavouring to explain what he was;
but seeing me approach he immediately poised his spear at
him, as being the nearest. Mr. Hume then unslung his
carbine, and presented it; but, as it was evident my re-
appearance had startled the savage, I pulled up; and he immediately lowered his weapon. His coolness and courage
surprised me, and increased my desire to communicate with
him. He had evidently taken both man and horse for one
animal, and as long as Mr. Hume kept his seat, the native
remained upon his guard; but when he saw him dismount,
after the first astonishment had subsided, he stuck his
spear into the ground, and walked fearlessly up to him.
We easily made him comprehend that we were in search of
water; when he pointed to the west, as indicating that we
should supply our wants there. He gave his information in

a frank and manly way, without the least embarrassment, and when the party passed, he stepped back to avoid the animals, without the smallest confusion. I am sure he was a very brave man; and I left him with the most favourable impressions, and not without hope that he would follow us.

From a more open forest, we entered a dense scrub, the soil in which was of a bright-red colour and extremely sandy, and the timber of various kinds. A leafless species of stenochylus aphylta, which, from the resemblance, I at first thought one of the polygonum tribe, was very abundant in the open spaces, and the young cypresses were occasionally so close as to turn us from the direction in which we had been moving. In the scrub we crossed Mr. Hume's tract, and, from the appearance of the ground, I was led to believe mine could not be very distant.

We struck upon a creek late in the afternoon, at which we stopped; New Year's Range bearing nearly due west at about four miles' distance. Had we struck upon my track, the question about which we were so anxious would still have been undecided; but the circumstance of our having crossed Mr. Hume's, which, from its direction, could not be mistaken, convinced me of the fate of the Macquarie, and I felt assured that, whatever channels it might have for the distribution of its waters, to the north of our line of route, the equality of surface of the interior would never permit it again to form a river; and that it only required an examination of the lower parts of the marshes to confirm the theory of the ultimate evaporation and absorption of its waters, instead

of their contributing to the permanence of an inland sea,
as Mr. Oxley had supposed.

On the 17th of January we encamped under New Year's
Range, which is the first elevation in the interior of Eastern
Australia to the westward of Mount Harris.   Yet when at
its base, I do not think that we had ascended above forty
feet higher than the plains in the neighbourhood of that
last mentioned eminence.   There certainly is a partial rise
of country, where the change of soil takes place from the
alluvial deposits of the marshes, to the sandy loam so
prevalent on the plains we had lately traversed; but I had
to regret that I was unable to decide so interesting a question by other than bare conjecture.

Notwithstanding that Mr. Hume had already been on
them, I encouraged hopes that a second survey of the
country from the highest point of New Year's Range,
would enable us to form some opinion of it, by which to
direct our future movements; but I was disappointed.

The two wooded hills I had seen from Oxley's Table
Land were visible from the range, bearing south; and
other eminences bore by compass S. W. and W. by S.; but
in every other direction the horizon was unbroken.   To the
westward, there appeared to be a valley of considerable extent, stretching N. and S., in which latter direction there
was a long strip of cleared ground, that looked very like
the sandy bed of a broad and rapid river.   The bare possi-
bility of the reality determined me to ascertain by inspec-
tion, whether my conjecture was right, and Mr. Hume

accompanied me on this excursion. After we left the camp we crossed a part of the range, and travelled for some time through open forest land that would afford excellent grazing in most seasons. We passed some hollows, and noticed many huts that had been occupied near them; but the hollows were now quite dry, and the huts had been long deserted. After about ten miles' ride we reached a plain of white sand, from which New Year's Range was distinctly visible; and this no doubt was the spot that had attracted my attention. Pools of water continued on it, from which circumstance it would appear that the sand had a substratum of clay or marl. From this plain we proceeded southerly through acacia scrub, bounding gently undulating forest land, and at length ascended some small elevations that scarcely deserved the name of hills. They had fragments of quartz profusely scattered over them; and the soil, which was sandy, contained particles of mica.

The view from them was confused, nor did any fresh object meet our observation. We had, however, considerably neared the two wooded hills, and the elevations that from the range were to the S. W., now bore N. W. of us. We had wandered too far from the camp to admit of our returning to it to sleep; we therefore commenced a search for water, and having found some, we tethered our horses near it for the night, and should have been tolerably comfortable, had not the mosquitoes been so extremely. troublesome. They defied the power of smoke, and annoyed me so much, that, hot as it was, I rolled myself in my boat

cloak, and perspired in consequence to such a degree, that
my clothes were wet through, and I had to stand at the fire
in the morning to dry them. Mr. Hume, who could not
bear such confinement, suffered the penalty, and was most
unmercifully bitten.

We reached the camp about noon the following day, and
learnt, to our vexation, that one of the men, Norman, had
lost himself shortly after we started, and had not since been
heard of.   Dawber, my overseer, was out in search of him.
I awaited his return, therefore, before I took any measures
for the man's recovery; nor was I without hopes that Dawber
would have found him, as it appeared he had taken one of
the horses with him, and Dawber, by keeping his tracks,
might eventually have overtaken him.   He returned, however, about 3 p.m. unsuccessful, when Mr. Hume and I
mounted our horses, and proceeded in different directions
in quest of him, but were equally disappointed.

We met at the creek in the dark, and returned to the
camp together, when I ordered the cypresses on the range
to be set on fire, and thus illuminated the country round
for many miles.   In the morning, however, as Norman had
not made his appearance, we again started in search of the
poor fellow, on whose account I was now most uneasy;
for his horse, it appeared, had escaped him, and was found
with the others at watering time.

I did not return to the camp until after sunset, more fatigued than I recollect ever having been before. I was,
however, rejoiced on being informed that the object of my

anxiety was safe in his tent; that he had caught sight of the hill the evening before, and that he had reached the camp shortly after I left it. He had been absent three nights and two days, and had not tasted water or food of any kind during that time.

To my enquiries he replied, that, being on horseback, he thought he could have overtaken a kangaroo, which passed him whilst waiting at the creek for the cattle, and that in the attempt, he lost himself. It would appear that he crossed the creek in the dark, and his horse escaped from him on the first night. He complained more of thirst than of hunger, although he had drunk at the watering-place to such an excess, on his return, as to make him vomit; but, though not a little exhausted, he had escaped better than I should have expected.

New Year's Range consists of a principal group of five hills, the loftiest of which does not measure 300 feet in height. It has lateral ridges, extending to the N. N. W. on the one hand, and bending in to the creek on the other. The former have a few cypresses, sterculia, and iron bark upon them; the latter are generally covered with brush, under box ; the brush for the most part consisting of two distinct species of stenochylus, and a new acacia. The whole range is of quartz formation, small fragments of which are profusely scattered over the ridges, and are abundantly incrusted with oxide of iron. The soil in the neighbourhood of New Year's Range is a red loam, with a slight mixture of sand. An open forest country lies between it and the creek, and it is not at all deficient in pasture.

That a change of soil takes place to the westward of the
creek, is obvious, from the change of vegetation, the most
remarkable feature of which is the sudden check given to the
further extension of the acacia pendula, which is not to be
found beyond it, it being succeeded by another acacia of the
same species and habits; neither do the plants of the chenopedia class exist in the immediate vicinity of the range.

I place these hills, as far as my observations will allow,
in east lon. 146° 32′ 15″, and in lat. 30° 21′ south; the
variation of the compass being 6° 40′ easterly.

As New Year's Creek was leading northerly, it had been
determined to trace it down as long as it should keep that
course, or one to the westward of it. We broke up the
camp, therefore, under the range, on the evening of the
18th, and moved to the creek, about two miles north of
the place at which we had before crossed it, with the
intention of prosecuting our journey on the morrow. But
both Mr. Hume and I were so fatigued that we were glad of
an opportunity to rest, even for a single day. We remained
stationary, therefore, on the 19th; nor was I without hope
that the natives whom we had surprised in the woods,
would have paid us a visit, since Mr. Hume had met
them in his search for Norman, and they had promised
not only to come to us, but to do all in their power to find
the man, whose footsteps some of them had crossed. They
did not, however, venture near us; and I rather attribute
their having kept aloof, to the circumstance of Mr. Hume's
having fired a shot, shortly after he left them, as a signal

to Norman, in the event of his being within hearing of the
report. They must have been alarmed at so unusual a
sound; but I am sure nothing was further from Mr. Hume's
intention than to intimidate them; his knowledge of their
manners and customs, as well as his partiality to the
natives, being equally remarkable. The circumstance is,
however, a proof of the great caution that is necessary in
communicating with them..

I have said that we remained stationary the day after
we left the range, with a view to enjoy a little rest;
it would, however, have been infinitely better if we had
moved forward. Our camp was infested by the kangaroo fly, which settled upon us in thousands. They appeared to rise from the ground, and as fast as they were
swept off were succeeded by fresh numbers. It was utterly
impossible to avoid their persecution, penetrating as they
did into the very tents.

The men were obliged to put handkerchiefs over their
faces, and stockings upon their hands; but they bit
through every thing. It was to no purpose that I myself
shifted from place to place; they still followed, or were
equally numerous everywhere. To add to our discomfort,
the animals were driven almost to madness, and galloped
to and fro in so furious a manner that I was apprehensive
some of them would have been lost. I never experienced
such a day of torment; and only when the sun set, did
these little creatures cease from their attacks.

It will be supposed that we did not stay to subject our-

selves to another trial; indeed it was with some degree of
horror that the men saw the first light of morning streak the
horizon. They got up immediately, and we moved down
the creek, on a northerly course, without breakfasting as
usual. We found that dense brushes of casuarina lined
the creek on both sides, beyond which, to our left, there
was open rising ground, on which eucalypti, cypresses, and
the acacia longifolia, prevailed; whilst to the east, plains
seemed to predominate.

Although we had left the immediate spot at which the
kangaroo flies (cabarus) seemed to be collected, I did not
expect that we should have got rid of them so completely
as we did. None of them were seen during the day; a
proof that they were entirely local. They were about half
the size of a common house fly, had flat brown bodies, and
their bite, although sharp and piercing, left no irritation
after it.

About noon we stopped at the creek side to take some
refreshment. The country bore an improved appearance
around us, and the cattle found abundance of pasture.
It was evident that the creek had been numerously frequented by the natives, although no recent traces of them
could be found. It had a bed of coarse red granite, of the
fragments of which the natives had constructed a weir
for the purpose of taking fish. The appearance of this
rock in so isolated a situation, is worthy the consideration
of geologists.

The promise of improvement I have noticed, gradually

disappeared as we proceeded on our day's journey, and
we at length found ourselves once more among brushes,
and on the edge of plains, over which the rhagodia prevailed. Nothing could exceed in dreariness the appearance
of the tracks through which we journeyed, on this and the
two following days.   The creek on which we depended for
a supply of water, gave such alarming indications of a
total failure, that I at one time, had serious thoughts of
abandoning my pursuit of it. We passed hollow after
hollow that had successively dried up, although originally
of considerable depth; and, when we at length found
water, it was doubtful how far we could make use of it.
Sometimes in boiling it left a sediment nearly equal to
half its body; at other times it was so bitter as to be
quite unpalatable.   That on which we subsisted was
scraped up from small puddles, heated by the sun's rays;
and so uncertain were we of finding water at the end of
the day's journey, that we were obliged to carry a supply
on one of the bullocks.   There was scarcely a living crea-
ture, even of the feathered race, to be seen to break the
stillness of the forest.   The native dogs alone wandered
about, though they had scarcely strength to avoid us;
and their melancholy howl, breaking in upon the ear at the
dead of the night, only served to impress more fully on
the mind the absolute loneliness of the desert.

It appeared, from their traces that the natives had
lingered on this ground, on which they had perhaps been
born, as long as it continued to afford them a scanty

though precarious subsistence ; but that they had at length
been forced from it.   Neither fish nor muscles remained in
the creek, nor emus nor kangaroos on the plains.   How
then could an European expect to find food in deserts
through which the savage wandered in vain ?   There is no
doubt of the fate that would have overtaken any one of the
party who might have strayed away, and I was happy to
find that Norman's narrow escape had made a due impression on the minds of his comrades.

We passed some considerable plains, lying to the eastward of the creek, on parts of which the grass, though
growing in tufts, was of luxuriant growth.   They were,
however, more generally covered with salsola and rhagodia,
and totally destitute of other vegetation, the soil upon them
being a red sandy loam.   The paths across the plains,
which varied in breadth from three to eight miles, were numerous; but they had not been recently trodden.   The
creek continued to have a thick brush of casuarina and
acacia near it, to the westward of which there was a rising
open forest track; the timber upon it being chiefly box,
cypress, and the acacia longifolia.   It was most probably
connected with New Year's Range, those elevations being
about thirty miles distant.   It terminated in some gentle
hills which, though covered in places with acacia shrub, were
sufficiently open to afford an extensive view.   From their
summit Oxley's Table Land, towards which we had been
gradually working our way, was distinctly visible, distant
about twenty miles, and bearing by compass W. by S.   On

descending from these hills,* which were scattered over with fragments of slaty quartz, we traversed a box flat, apparently subject to overflow, having a barren sandy scrub to its left. I had desired the men to preserve a W. N. W. direction, on leaving them, supposing that that course would have kept them near the creek; but, on overtaking the party, I found that they had wandered completely away from it. The fact was, that the creek had taken a sudden bend to the eastward of N. and had thus thrown them out. It was with some difficulty that we regained it before sunset; and we were at length obliged to stop for the night at a small plain, about a quarter of a mile short of it, but we had the satisfaction of having excellent feed for the animals.

Fearful that New Year's Creek would take us too far to the eastward, and being anxious to keep westward as much as possible, it struck me that we could not, under existing circumstances, do better than make for Oxley's Table Land. Water, I knew, we should find in a swamp at it's base, and we might discover some more encouraging feature than I had observed on my hasty visit to it. We left the creek, therefore on the 23d, and once more took up a westerly course. Passing through a generally open country, we stopped at noon to rest the animals; and afterwards got on an excellent grazing forest track, which continued to the brush, through another part of which I had penetrated to the marsh more to the south. While making our way through it, we came upon a small pond of water, and must

* Called the Pink Hills, from the colour of a flower found upon them.

have alarmed some natives, as there was a fresh made fire
close to it. Our journey had been unusually long, and the
cattle had felt the heat so much, that the moment they saw
water they rushed into it; and, as this created some confusion, I thought it best to stop where we were for the night.

In the morning, Mr. Hume walked with me to the hill,
a distance of about a mile. It is not high enough to deserve the name of a mountain, although a beautiful feature
in the country, and showing well from any point of view.
We ascended it with an anxiety that may well be imagined,
but were wholly disappointed in our most sanguine expectations. Our chief object, in this second visit to Oxley's
Table Land, had been to examine, more at leisure, the face
of the country around it, and to discover, if possible, some
fixed point on which to move.

If the rivers of the interior had already exhausted themselves, what had we to expect from a creek whose diminished appearance where we left it made us apprehend its
speedy termination, and whose banks we traversed under
constant apprehension? In any other country I should
have followed such a water course, in hopes of its ultimately leading to some reservoir; but here I could encourage no such favourable anticipation.

The only new object that struck our sight was a remarkable and distant hill of conical shape, bearing by compass
S. 10 E. To the southward and westward, in the direction
of D'Urban's Group, a dense and apparently low brush
extended; but to the N. and N.W., there was a regular

alternation of wood and plain.   I left Mr. Hume upon the
hill, that he might the more readily notice any smoke made
by the natives; and returned myself to the camp about one
o'clock, to move the party to the swamp. Mr. Hume's perseverance was of little avail.   The region he had been
overlooking was, to all appearance, uninhabited, nor did a
single fire indicate that there was even a solitary wanderer
upon its surface.

Our situation, at this time, was extremely embarrassing,
and the only circumstance on which we had to congratulate
ourselves was, the improved condition of our men; for
several of the cattle and horses were in a sad plight. The
weather had been so extremely oppressive, that we had
found it impossible to keep them free from eruptions.
I proposed to Mr. Hume, therefore, to give them a few
days' rest, and to make an excursion, with such of them as
were serviceable, to D'Urban's Group.   We were both of
us unwilling to return to the creek, but we foresaw that a
blind reliance upon fortune, in our next movements, might
involve us in inextricable difficulty.

On the other hand, there was a very great risk in delay.
It was more than probable, from the continued drought,
that our retreat would be cut off from the want of water,
or that we should only be enabled to effect our retreat with
loss of most of the animals. The hope, however, of our in-
tersecting some stream, or of falling upon a better country,
prevailed over other considerations; and the excursion was,
consequently, determined upon.

We left the camp on the 25th, accompanied by Hopkinson and the tinker; and, almost immediately after, entered an acacia scrub of the most sterile description, and one, through which it would have been impossible to have found a passage for the boat carriage. The soil was almost a pure sand, and the lower branches of the trees were decayed so generally as to give the whole an indescribable appearance of desolation. About mid-day, we crossed a light sandy plain, on which there were some dirty puddles of water. They were so shallow as to leave the backs of the frogs in them exposed, and they had, in consequence, been destroyed by solar heat, and were in a state of putrefaction. Our horses refused to drink, but it was evident that some natives must have partaken of this sickening beverage only a few hours before our arrival. Indeed, it was clear that a wandering family must have slept near this spot, as we observed a fresh made gunneah (or native hut), and their foot-prints were so fresh along the line we were pursuing, that we momentarily expected to have overtaken them. It was late in the evening when we got out of this brush into better and more open ground, where, in ordinary seasons we should, no doubt, have found abundance of water. But we now searched in vain for it, and were contented to be enabled to give our wearied animals better food than they had tasted for many days, the forest grass, though in tufts, being abundant.

We brought up for the night at the edge of a scrub, having travelled from thirty-two to thirty-five miles, judging

THE CRESTED PIGEON OF THE MARSHES.

'ublished by Smith, Elder & C? Cornhill, London

the distance from the mountains still to be about twelve.

In the morning we started at an early hour, and immediately entered the brush, beneath which we had slept; pursuing a westerly course through it. After a short ride, we found ourselves upon a plain, that was crowded with flocks of cockatoos. Here we got a supply of water, such as it was — so mixed with slime as to hang in strings between the fingers; and, after a hasty breakfast, we proceeded on our journey, mostly through a barren sandy scrub that was a perfect burrow from the number of wombats in it, to within a mile of the hill group, where the country appeared like one continuous meadow to the very base of them. I never saw anything like the luxuriance of the grass on this tract of country, waving as it did higher than our horses' middles as we rode through it. We ascended the S.W. face of the mountain to an elevation of at least 800 feet above the level of the plain, and had some difficulty in scaling the masses of rock that opposed themselves to our progress. But on gaining the summit, we were amply repaid for our trouble. The view extended far and wide, but we were again disappointed in the main object that had induced us to undertake the journey. I took the following bearings by compass. Oxley's Table Land bore N. 40 E. distant forty-five miles; small and distant hill due E.; conical peak seen from Oxley's Table Land S. 60 E., very distant; long ridge of high land, S.E., distant thirty-five miles; high land, S. 30 E., distant thirty miles; long range, S. 25 W.

To the westward, as a medium point, the horizon was unbroken, and the eye wandered over an apparently endless succession of wood and plain.   A brighter green than usual marked the course of the mountain torrents in several places, but there was no glittering light among the trees, no smoke to betray a water hole, or to tell that a single inhabitant was traversing the extensive region we were overlooking.   We were obliged to return to the plain on which we had breakfasted, and to sleep upon it.

D'Urban's Group is of compact sandstone formation. Its extreme length is from E. S. E. to W. N. W., and cannot be more than from seven to nine miles, whilst its breadth is from two to four.   The central space forms a large basin, in which there are stinted pines and eucalyptus scrub, amid huge fragments of rocks.   It rises like an island from the midst of the ocean, and as I looked upon it from the plains below, I could without any great stretch of the imagination, picture to myself that it really was such. Bold and precipitous, it only wanted the sea to lave its base; and I cannot but think that such must at no very remote period have been the case, and that the immense flat we had been traversing, is of comparatively recent formation.

We reached the camp on the 28th of the month, by nearly the same route; and were happy to find that, after the few days' rest they had enjoyed, there was a considerable improvement in the animals.

Our experience of the nature of the country to the south-

ward, and the westward, was such as to deter us from risk-
ing anything, by taking such a direction as was most
agreeable to our views. Nothing remained to us but to
follow the creek, or to retreat; and as we could only be
induced to adopt the last measure when every other expedient should have failed, we determined on pursuing our original plan, of tracing New Year's Creek as far as practicable.

Oxley's Table Land is situated in lat. 29° 57' 30", and in E.
long. 145° 43' 30", the mean variation being 6. 32 easterly.
It consists of two hills that appear to have been rent
asunder by some convulsion of nature, since the passage
between them is narrow and their inner faces are equally
perpendicular. The hill which I have named after the late
Surveyor-general, is steep on all sides; but the other gradually declines from the south, and at length loses itself in
a large plain that extends to the north. It is from four to five
miles in length, and is picturesque in appearance, and
lightly wooded. A few cypresses were growing on Oxley's
Table Land; but it had, otherwise, very little timber upon its
summit. Both hills are of sandstone formation, and there
are some hollows upon the last that deserve particular notice. They have the appearance of having been formed by
eddies of water, being deeper in the centre than at any other
part, and contain fragments and slabs of sandstone of various
size and breadth, without a particle of soil or of sand
between them. It is to be observed that the edges of these
slabs, which were perfect parallelograms, were unbroken,
and that they were as clean as if they had only just been

turned out of the hand of the mason. We counted thirteen
of these hollows in one spot about twenty-five feet in diame-
ter, but they are without doubt of periodical formation,
since a single hollow was observed lower than the summit of
the hill upon its south extremity, that had evidently long
been exposed to the action of the atmosphere, and had a
general coating of moss over it.

We left Oxley's Table Land on the morning of the 31st of
January, pursuing a northern course through the brush and
across a large plain, moving parallel to the smaller hill,
and keeping it upon our left. The soil upon this plain
differed in character from that on the plains to the eastward, and was much freer from sand. We stopped to dine
at a spot, whence Oxley's Table Land bore by compass,
S. by W., distant about twelve miles. Continuing our
journey, at 2 p. m. we cleared the plain, and entered a
tract covered with the polygonum junceum, on a soil
evidently the deposit of floods. Box-trees were thinly
scattered over it, and among the polygonum, the crested
pigeons were numerous. These general appearances, together with a dip of country to the N. N. W., made us conclude that we were approaching the creek, and we accordingly intersected it on a N. N. E. course, at about three
miles' distance from where we had dined. It had, however, undergone so complete a change, and had increased
so much in size and in the height of its banks, that we were
at a loss to recognize it. Still, with all these favourable
symptoms, there was not a drop of water in it. But small

shells lay in heaps in its bed, or were abundantly scattered over it; and we remarked that they differed from those on the plains of the Macquarie. A circumstance that surprised us much, was the re-appearance of the flooded-gum upon its banks, and that too of a large size. We had not seen any to the westward of the marshes, and we were, consequently, led to indulge in more sanguine expectation as to our ulti- mate success than we had ever ventured to do before.

The party crossed to the right bank of the creek, and then moved in a westerly direction along it in search of water. A brush extended to our right, and some broken stony ground, rather elevated, was visible, to which Mr. Hume rode; nor did he join me again until after I had halted the party for the night.

My search for water had been unsuccessful, and the sun had set, when I came upon a broad part of the creek that appeared very favourable for an encampment, as it was en- compassed by high banks, and would-afford the men a greater facility of watching the cattle, that I knew would stray away if they could.

My anxiety for them led me to wander down the bed of the creek, when, to my joy, I found a pond of water within a hundred yards of the tents. It is impossible for me to describe the relief I felt at this success, or the glad- ness it spread among the men. Mr. Hume joined me at dusk, and informed me that he had made a circuit, and had struck upon the creek about three miles below us but that, in tracing it up, he had not found a drop of water

until he came to the pond near which we had so providentially encamped.   On the following morning, we held a
westerly course over an open country for about eight miles
and a half.   The prevailing timber appeared to be a species
of eucalypti, with -rough bark, of small size, and evidently
languishing from the want of moisture.   The soil over which
we travelled was far from bad, but there was a total absence
of water upon it.   At 6 p.m. Oxley's Table Land was distant from us about fifteen miles, bearing S. 20 E. by compass.

We had not touched upon the creek from the time we left
it in the morning, having wandered from it in a northerly
direction, along a native path that we intersected, and
that seemed to have been recently trodden, since footsteps
were fresh upon it.   At sunset, we crossed a broad dry creek
that puzzled us extremely, and were shortly afterwards
obliged to stop for the night upon a plain beyond it.   We
had, during the afternoon, bent down to the S. W. in hopes
that we should again have struck upon New Year's Creek ;
and, under an impression that we could not be far from it,
Mr. Hume and I walked across the plain, to ascertain if it
was sufficiently near to be of any service to us.   We came
upon a creek, but could not decide whether it was the one
for which we had been searching, or another.

Its bed was so perfectly even that it was impossible to
say to what point it flowed, more especially as all remains of
debris had mouldered away.   It was, however, extremely
broad, and evidently, at times, held a furious torrent.   In
the centre of it, at one of the angles, we discovered a pole

erected, and at first thought, from the manner in which it
was propped up, that some unfortunate European must
have placed it there as a mark to tell of his wanderings, but
we afterwards concluded that it might be some superstitious
rite of the natives, in consequence of the untowardness of
the season, as it seemed almost inconceivable that an European could have wandered to such a distance from the
located districts in safety.

The creek had flooded-gum growing upon its banks,
and, on places apparently subject to flood, a number of tall
straight saplings were observed by us. We returned to the
camp, after a vain search for water, and were really at a loss
what direction next to pursue. The men kept the cattle
pretty well together, and, as we were not delayed by any
preparations for breakfast, they were saddled and loaded at
an early hour. The circumstance of there having been natives in the neighbourhood, of whom we had seen so few
traces of late, assured me that water was at hand, but in
what direction it was impossible to guess. As the path
we had observed was leading northerly, we took up that
course, and had not proceeded more than a mile upon it,
when we suddenly found ourselves on the banks of a noble
river. Such it might in truth be called, where water was
scarcely to be found. The party drew up upon a bank
that was from forty to forty-five feet above the level of the
stream. The channel of the river was from seventy to
eighty yards broad, and enclosed an unbroken sheet of
water, evidently very deep, and literally covered with pe-

licans and other wild fowl. Our surprise and delight may
better be imagined than described. Our difficulties seemed
to be at an end, for here was a river that promised to reward all our exertions, and which appeared every moment to
increase in importance to our imagination. Coming from the
N. E., and flowing to the S.W., it had a capacity of channel
that proved that we were as far from its source as from its
termination. The paths of the natives on either side of it
were like well trodden roads; and the trees that overhung
it were of beautiful and gigantic growth.

Its banks were too precipitous to allow of our watering the cattle, but the men eagerly descended to quench
their thirst, which a powerful sun had contributed to
increase; nor shall I ever forget the cry of amazement that
followed their doing so, or the looks of terror and dis-
appointment with which they called out to inform me that
the water was so salt as to be unfit to drink! This was,
indeed, too true: on tasting it, I found it extremely nauseous, and strongly impregnated with salt, being apparently
a mixture of sea and fresh water. Whence this arose, whether from local causes, or from a communication with some
inland sea, I knew not, but the discovery was certainly a
blow for which I was not prepared. Our hopes were annihilated at the moment of their apparent realization. The
cup of joy was dashed out of our hands before we had
time to raise it to our lips. Notwithstanding this disap-
pointment, we proceeded down the river, and halted at
about five miles, being influenced by the goodness of the

feed to provide for the cattle as well as circumstances would permit. They would not drink of the river water, but stood covered in it for many hours, having their noses alone exposed above the stream. Their condition gave me great uneasiness. It was evident they could not long hold out under their excessive thirst, and unless we should procure some fresh water, it would be impossible for us to continue our journey. On a closer examination, the river appeared to me much below its ordinary level, and its current was scarcely perceptible. We placed sticks to ascertain if there was a rise or fall of tide, but could arrive at no satisfactory conclusion, although there was undoubtedly a current in it. Yet, as I stood upon its banks at sunset, when not a breath of air existed to break the stillness of the waters below me, and saw their surface kept in constant agitation by the leaping of fish, I doubted whether the river could supply itself so abundantly, and the rather imagined, that it owed such abundance, which the pelicans seemed to indicate was constant, to some mediterranean sea or other. Where, however, were the human inhabitants of this distant and singular region? The signs of a numerous population were around us, but we had not seen even a solitary wanderer. The water of the river was not, by any means, so salt as that of the ocean, but its taste was precisely similar. Could it be that its unnatural state had driven its inhabitants from its banks?

One would have imagined that our perplexities would have been sufficient for one day, but ere night closed,

they increased upon us, although our anxiety, with regard to the cattle, was happily removed. Mr. Hume,
with his usual perseverance, walked out when the camp
was formed; and, at a little distance from it, ascended a
ridge of pure sand, crowned with cypresses. From this,
he descended to the westward, and, at length, struck upon
the river, where a reef of rocks crossed its channel, and
formed a dry passage from one side to the other; but the
bend, which the river must have taken, appeared to him
so singular, that he doubted whether it was the same
beside which we had been travelling during the day.
Curiosity led him to cross it, when he found a small pond
of fresh water on a tongue of land, and, immediately afterwards, returned to acquaint me with the welcome tidings.
It was too late to move, but we had, at least, the prospect
of a comfortable breakfast in the morning.

In consequence of the doubts that hung upon Mr. Hume's
mind, as to the course of the river, we arranged that the
animals should precede us to the fresh water; and that we
should keep close in upon the stream, to ascertain that
point. After traversing a deep bight, we arrived nearly as
soon as the party, at the appointed rendezvous. The
rocks composing the channel of the river at the crossing
place, were of indurated clay. In the course of an hour,
the animals appearing quite refreshed, we proceeded on our
journey, and at about four miles crossed New Year's Creek, at
its junction with the salt river. We passed several parts of the
main channel that were perfectly dry, and were altogether

at a loss to account for the current we undoubtedly had
observed in the river when we first came upon it.   At mid-
day D'Urban's Group bore S. 65 E. distant about 32 miles.
We made a little westing in the afternoon.   The river continued to maintain its character and appearance, its lofty
banks, and its long still reaches: while, however, the blue-
gum trees upon its banks were of magnificent size, the soil
had but little vegetation upon it, although an alluvial deposit.

We passed over vast spaces covered with the polygonum
junceum, that bore all the appearance of the flooded
tracks in the neighbourhood of the marshes, and on which
the travelling was equally distressing to the animals.   Indeed, it had been sufficiently evident to us that the waters
of this river were not always confined to its channel, capacious as it was, but that they inundated a belt of barren
land, that varied in width from a quarter of a mile to a
mile, when they were checked by an outer embankment
that prevented them from spreading generally over the
country, and upon the neighbouring plains.   At our halting
place, the cattle drank sparingly of the water, but it acted
as a violent purgative both on them and the men who partook of it.

On the 5th, the river led us to the southward and westward.   Early in the day, we passed a group of seventy
huts, capable of holding from twelve to fifteen men each.
They appeared to be permanent habitations, and all of
them fronted the same point of the compass.   In searching
amongst them we observed two beautifully made nets, of

about ninety yards in length. The one had much larger meshes than the other, and was, most probably, intended to take kangaroos; but the other was evidently a fishing net.

In one hut, the floor of which was swept with particular care, a number of white balls, as of pulverised shells or lime, had been deposited — the use of which we could not divine. A trench was formed round the hut to prevent the rain from running under it, and the whole was arranged with more than ordinary attention.

We had not proceeded very far when we came suddenly upon the tribe to which this village, as it might be called, belonged.

In breaking through some brush to an open space that was bounded on one side by the river, we observed three or four natives, seated on a bank at a considerable distance from us; and directly in the line on which we were moving. The nature of the ground so completely favoured our approach, that they did not become aware of it until we were within a few yards of them, and had ascended a little ridge, which, as we afterwards discovered, ended in an abrupt precipice upon the river, not more than thirty yards to our right. The crack of the drayman's whip was the first thing that aroused their attention. They gazed upon us for a moment, and then started up and assumed an attitude of horror and amazement; their terror apparently increasing upon them. We stood perfectly immoveable, until at length they gave a fearful yell, and darted out of sight.

Their cry brought about a dozen more natives from the river, whom we had not before observed, but who now ran after their comrades with surprising activity, and without once venturing to look behind them. As our position was a good one, we determined to remain upon it, until we should ascertain the number and disposition of the natives. We had not been long stationary, when we heard a crackling noise in the distance, and it soon became evident that the bush had been fired. It was, however, impossible that we could receive any injury on the narrow ridge upon which we stood, so that we waited very patiently to see the end of this affair.

In a short time the fire approached pretty near to us, and dense columns of smoke rose into the air over our heads. One of the natives, who had been on the bank, now came out of the bush, exactly from the spot into which he had retreated. He advanced a few paces towards us, and bending his body so that his hands rested on his knees, he fixed his gaze upon us for some time; but, seeing that we remained immoveable, he began to throw himself into the most extravagant attitudes, shaking his foot from time to time. When he found that all his violence had no effect, he turned his rear to us in a most laughable manner, and absolutely groaned in spirit when he found that this last insult failed of success.

He stood perplexed and not knowing what next to do, which gave Mr. Hume an opportunity to call out to him, and with considerable address he at length got the savage to approach close up to him; Mr. Hume himself having advanced a short distance from the animals in the first instance. As soon as I thought the savage had sufficiently recovered from his alarm, I went up to him with a tomahawk, the use of which he immediately guessed. We now observed that the natives who had fled from the river, had been employed in setting a net. They had placed it in a semicircle, with either end to the shore, and rude pieces of wood were attached to it to keep the upper part perpendicular. It was in fact a sein, only that the materials, with the exception of the net-work, were simpler and rougher than cork or lead — for which last, we afterwards discovered stones had been substituted.

We had on this occasion a remarkable instance of the docility of the natives of the interior, or of the power they have of subduing their apprehensions; manifesting the opposite extremes of fear and confidence. These men whom we had thus surprised, and who, no doubt, imagined that we were about to destroy them, having apparently never seen nor heard of white men before, must have taken us for something preternatural; yet from the extremity of fear that had prompted them to set their woods in flames, they in a brief space so completely subdued those fears as to approach the very beings who had so strongly excited their alarm. The savage who had been the principal actor in the scene, was an elderly man, rather descending to the vale of years than what might be strictly called aged. I know not how it was, but I regarded him with peculiar interest. Mr.

Hume's manners had in a great measure contributed to allay his evident agitation; but, from the moment I approached him, I thought there was a shade of anxiety upon his brow, and an expression of sorrow over his features, the cause of which did not originate with us. I could see in a moment, that his bosom was full even to bursting, and he seemed to claim at once our sympathy and our protection, although we were ignorant of that which oppressed him. We had not long been seated together, when some of his tribe mustered sufficient courage to join him. Both Mr. Hume and I were desirous of seeing the net drawn, but the old man raised some objection, by pointing to the heavens and towards the sun. After a little more solicitation, however, he gave a whistle, and, four or five natives having obeyed the summons, he directed them to draw the net, but they were unfortunate, and our wish to ascertain the kind of fish contained in the river was disappointed. As his tribe gathered round him, the old chief threw a melancholy glance upon them, and endeavoured, as much as he could, to explain the cause of that affliction which, as I had rightly judged, weighed heavily upon him. It appeared, then, that a violent cutaneous disease raged throughout the tribe, that was sweeping them off in great numbers. He called several young men to Mr. Hume and myself, who had been attacked by this singular malady. Nothing could exceed the anxiety of his explanations, or the mild and soothing tone in which he addressed his people, and it really pained me that I could not assist him in his distress. We now discovered the use to which the conical substance that had been deposited with such unusual care in one of the huts, was applied. There were few of the natives present who were not more or less marked with it, and it was no doubt, indicative of mourning.

Some of the men, however, were painted with red and yellow ochre, with which it was evident to me they had besmeared themselves since our appearance, most likely in preparing for the combat in which they fancied they would be engaged. We distributed such presents as we had to those around us, and when we pursued our journey, the majority accompanied us, nor did they wholly leave us until we had passed the place to which their women had retired. They might have left us when they pleased, for we intended them no harm ; as it was, however, they struck into the brushes to join their families, and we pushed on to make up for lost time.

The travelling near the river had been so bad, not only in consequence of the nature of the soil and brush, but from the numerous gullies that had been formed by torrents, as they poured into its channel after heavy rains and floods, that it was thought advisable to keep at a greater distance from it. We turned away, therefore, to the plains, and found them of much firmer surface. They partook, however, of the same general character as the plains we had traversed more to the eastward. Their soil was a light sandy loam, and the same succulent plants still continued to prevail upon them, which we have already noticed as existing upon the other plains. Both emus and kangaroos were seen, though not in any considerable numbers, but our dogs were not in a condition to run, and were all but killed by the extreme heat of the weather. We had fallen on a small pool of water shortly after we started in the morning, but we could do no more than refresh ourselves and the animals at it. In the afternoon, we again turned towards the river, and found it unaltered. Its water was still salt, and from the increased number of wild fowl and pelicans upon it, as well as from the general flatness of the country, I certainly thought we were rapidly approaching some inland sea. It was, however, uncertain how long we should be enabled to continue on the river. The animals were all of them extremely weak, and every day increased the probable difficulty of our return. There was not the least appearance of a break-up of the drought, the heavens were without a cloud, and the atmosphere was so clear that the outline of the moon could be distinctly seen, although she was far in her wane.

On the 6th, we journeyed again through a barren scrub, although on firmer ground, and passed numerous groups of huts. At about eight miles from our last encampment, we came upon the river, where its banks were of considerable height. In riding along them, Mr. Hume thought he observed a current running, and he called to inform me of the circumstance. On a closer examination, we discovered some springs in the very bed of the river, from which a considerable stream was gushing, and from the incrustation around them, we had no difficulty in guessing at their nature : in fact, they were brine springs, and I collected a quantity of salt from the brink of them.

After such a discovery, we could not hope to keep our position. No doubt the current we had observed on first reaching the river, was caused by springs that had either escaped our notice or were under water. Here was at length a local cause for its saltness that destroyed at once the anticipation and hope of our being near its termination, and, consequently, the ardour with which we should have pressed on to decide so interesting a point.

Our retreat would have been a measure of absolute necessity ere this, had we not found occasional supplies of fresh water, the last pond of which was now about eighteen miles behind us.

Whether we should again find any, was a doubtful question, and I hesitated to run the risk. The animals were already, from bad food, and from the effects of the river water, so weak, that they could scarcely carry their loads, and I was aware, if any of the bullocks once fell, he would never rise again. Under such circumstances, I thought it better to halt the party at the edge of the scrub, though the feed was poor, and the water not drinkable. Our situation required most serious consideration. It was necessary that we should move either backward or forward in the morning. Yet we could not adopt either measure with satisfaction to ourselves, under such unfavorable circumstances. I determined to relieve my own mind by getting the animals into a place of safety, as soon as possible; and, as the only effectual way of doing this was to retire upon the nearest fresh water, I resolved at once to do so. The party turned back on the morning of the 6th; nor do I think the cattle would ever have reached their destination had we not found a few buckets of rain water in the cleft of a rock, to refresh them. Thus it will appear that under our most trying circumstances, we received aid from Providence, and that the bounty of Heaven was extended towards us, when we had least reason to expect it.

Notwithstanding we had been thus forced to a partial retreat, both Mr. Hume and myself were unwilling to quit the pursuit of the river, in so unsatisfactory a manner. There was no difference in the appearance of the country to the westward of it; but a seeming interminable flat stretched away in that direction. A journey across it was not likely, therefore, to be attended with any favorable results, since it was improbable that any other leading feature was within our reach. I proposed, therefore, to take the most serviceable of the horses with me down the river, that, in the event of our finding fresh water, we might again push forward. Mr. Hume requesting to be permitted to accompany me, it was arranged that we should start on the 8th, thereby giving the animals a day's rest. We had not seen any natives since our parting with the chief horde; and as we were stationed at some little distance from the river, I hoped that they would not visit the camp during my absence. This was the only circum-

stance that gave me uneasiness, but the men had generally
been behaving so well that I relied a great deal upon them.

About 3 p. m. on the 7th, Mr. Hume and I were occupied tracing the chart upon the ground. The day had
been remarkably fine, not a cloud was there in the heavens,
nor a breath of air to be felt. On a sudden we heard what
seemed to be the report of a gun fired at the distance of
between five and six miles. It was not the hollow sound of
an earthly explosion, or the sharp cracking noise of falling
timber, but in every way resembled a discharge of a
heavy piece of ordnance. On this all were agreed, but no
one was certain whence the sound proceeded. Both
Mr. Hume and myself had been too attentive to our
occupation to form a satisfactory opinion; but we both
thought it came from the N. W. I sent one of the men
immediately up a tree, but he could observe nothing unusual. The country around him appeared to be equally
flat on all sides, and to be thickly wooded: whatever
occasioned the report, it made a strong impression on all
of us; and to this day, the singularity of such a sound,
in such a situation, is a matter of mystery to me.

On the 8th, we commenced our journey down the river,
accompanied by two men, and a pack-horse, carrying our
provisions on one side and a bucket of water on the other.
Keeping in general near the stream, but making occasional
turns into the plains, we got to the brush from which the
party had turned back, about 3 p. m. Passing through,
we crossed a small plain, of better soil and vegetation

than usual; but it soon gave place to the sandy loam of
the interior; nor did we observe any material alteration,
either in the country or the river, as we rode along. The
flooded-gum trees on the banks of the latter, were of
beautiful growth, but in the brushes dividing the plains,
box and other eucalypti, with cypresses and many minor
shrubs, prevailed. We slept on the river side, and calculated our distance from the camp at about twenty-six
or twenty-eight miles.

The horses would not drink the river water, so that we
were obliged to give them a pint each from our own supply.
On the following morning we continued our journey. The
country was generally open to the eastward, and we had
fine views of D'Urban's Group, distant from twenty to
twenty-five miles. About noon, turning towards the river
to rest, both ourselves and the horses, we passed through
brush land for about a mile and a half. When we came
upon its banks, we found them composed of a red loam
with sandy superficies. We had, in the course of the day,
crossed several creeks, but in none of them could we find
water, although their channels were of great depth.

The day had been extremely warm, and from shaking in
the barrel our supply of water had diminished to a little more
than a pint; it consequently became a matter of serious consideration, how far it would be prudent to proceed farther;
for, however capable we were of bearing additional fatigue,
it was evident our animals would soon fail, since they
trembled exceedingly, and had the look of total exhaustion.

We calculated that we were forty miles from the camp, in a S. W. direction, a fearful distance under our circumstances, since we could not hope to obtain relief for two days. Independently however, of the state of the animals, our spirits were damped by the nature of the country, and the change which had taken place on the soil, upon which it was impossible that water could rest; while the general appearance of the interior shewed how much it had suffered from drought. On the other hand, although the waters of the river had become worse to the taste, the river itself had increased in size, and stretched away to the westward, with all the uniformity of a magnificent canal, and gave every promise of increasing importance; while the pelicans were in such numbers upon it as to be quite dazzling to the eye. Considering, however, that perseverance would only involve us in inextricable difficulties, and that it would also be useless to risk the horses, since we had gained a distance to which the bullocks could not have been brought, I intimated my intention of giving up the further pursuit of the river, though it was with extreme reluctance that I did so.

As soon as we had bathed and finished our scanty meal, I took the bearings of D'Urban's Group, and found them to be S. 58 E. about thirty-three miles distant; and as we mounted our horses, I named the river the " Darling," as a lasting memorial of the respect I bear the governor.

I should be doing injustice to Mr. Hume and my men,

if I did not express my conviction that they were extremely unwilling to yield to circumstances, and that, had I determined on continuing the journey, they would have followed me with cheerfulness, whatever the consequences might have been.

CHAPTER III.

WE kept near the river as we journeyed homewards, and in striking across a plain, found an isolated rock of quartz and jasper, just shewing itself partially above the surface of the ground.

We were anxious to get to the small plain I have mentioned, if possible, for the sake of the animals, and pushed on rapidly for it. About 4 p. m. we had reached our sleeping place of the previous evening, and being overpowered by thirst, we stopped in hopes that by making our tea strong we might destroy, in some measure, the nauseous taste of the water. The horses were spancelled and a fire lit. Whilst we were sitting patiently for the boiling of the tins, Mr. Hume observed at a considerable distance above us, a large body of natives under some gum trees. They were not near enough for us to observe them distinctly, but it was evident that they were watching our motions. We did not take any notice of them for some time, but at last I thought it better to call out to them, and accordingly requested Mr. Hume to do so. In a moment the whole of them ran forward and dashed into the river, having been on the opposite side, with an uproar I had never witnessed on any former occasion.

Mr. Hume thought they intended an attack, and the horses had taken fright and galloped away. I determined, therefore, to fire at once upon them if they pressed up the bank on which we were posted. Mr. Hume went with me to the crest of it, and we rather angrily beckoned to the foremost of the natives to stop. They mistook our meaning, but laid all their spears in a heap as they came up. We then sat down on the bank and they immediately did the same; nor did they stir until we beckoned to them after the horses had been secured.

As they conducted themselves so inoffensively, we gave them everything we had to spare. My gun seemed to excite their curiosity, as they had seen Mr. Hume shoot a cockatoo with it; they must consequently have been close to us for the greater part of the day, as the bird was killed in the morning. It was of a species new to me, being smaller than the common white cockatoo, and having a large scarlet-and-yellow instead of a pine-yellow top-knot.

Having staid about half an hour with them, we re-mounted our horses, and struck away from the river into the plains, while the natives went up its banks to join their hordes. Those whom we saw were about twenty-seven in number and the most of them were strangers.

It was some time after sunset before we reached the little plain on which we had arranged to sleep, and when we dismounted we were in a truly pitiable state. I had been unable to refrain from drinking copiously at the river, and now became extremely sick. Mr. Hume had been scarcely more prudent than myself, but on him the water had a contrary effect, as well as upon Hopkinson. The tinker was the only man fit for duty, and it was well for us that such was the case, as the horses made frequent attempts to stray, and would have left us in a pretty plight had they succeeded. We reached the camp on the following day a little before sunset, nor was I more rejoiced to dismount from my wearied horse than to learn that everything in the camp had been regular during our absence, and that the men had kept on the best terms with the natives, who had paid them frequent visits.

The bullocks had improved, but were still extremely weak, and as the horses we had employed on the last jour-ney required a day or two's rest, it was arranged that we should not break up our camp until the 12th, beyond which period we could not stop, in consequence of the low state of our salt provisions, we having barely sufficient to last to Mount Harris, at the rate of two pounds per week.

The morning after we returned from our excursion, a large party of natives, about seventy in number, visited the camp. On this occasion, the women and children passed behind the tents, but did not venture to stop. Most of the men had spears, and were unusually inquisitive and forward. Several of them carried fire-sticks under the influence of the disease I have already noticed, whilst others were remarked to have violent cutaneous eruptions all over the body. We were pretty well on the alert; notwithstanding which, every minor article was seized with a quickness that would have done credit to a most finished juggler. One of the natives thus picked up my comb and tooth-brush, but as he did not attempt to conceal them, they were fortunately recovered. After staying with us a short time the men followed the women. They appeared to be strangers who had come from a distance.

The natives of the Darling are a clean-limbed, well-conditioned race, generally speaking. They seemingly occupy permanent huts, but their tribe did not bear any proportion to the size or number of their habitations. It was evident their population had been thinned. The customs of these distant tribes, as far as we could judge, were similar to those of the mountain blacks, and they are essentially the same people, although their language differs. They lacerate their bodies, but do not extract the front teeth. We saw but few cloaks among them, since the opossum does not inhabit the interior. Those that were noticed, were made of the red kangaroo skin. In appearance, these men are stouter in the bust than at the lower extremities; they have broad noses, sunken eyes, overhanging eyebrows, and thick lips. The men are much better looking than the women. Both go perfectly naked, if I except the former, who wear nets over the loins and across the forehead, and bones through the cartilages of the nose. Their chief food is fish, of which they have great supplies in the river; still they have their seasons for hunting their emus and kangaroos. The nets they use for this purpose, as well as for fishing, are of great length, and are made upon large frames. These people do not appear to have warlike habits, nor do they take any pride in their arms, which differ little from those used by the inland tribes, and are assimilated to them as far as the materials will allow. One powerful man, however, had a regular trident, for which Mr. Hume offered many things without success. He plainly intimated to us that he had a use for it, but whether against an enemy or to secure prey, we could not understand. I was most anxious to have ascertained if any religious ceremonies obtained among them, but the difficulty of making them comprehend our meaning was insurmountable; and to the same cause may be attributed the circumstance of my being unable to collect any satisfactory vocabulary of their language. They evinced a strange perversity, or obstinacy rather, in repeating words, although it was evident that they knew they were meant as questions. The pole we observed in the creek, on the evening previously to our making the Darling, was not the only one that fell under our notice ; our impression therefore, that they were fixed by the natives to propitiate some deity, was confirmed. It would appear that the white pigment was an indication of mourning. Whether these people have an idea of a superintending Providence I doubt, but they evidently dread evil agency. On the whole I should say they are a people, at present, at the very bottom of the scale of humanity.

We struck the Darling River in lat. 29° 37′ S. and in E. long. 145° 33′, and traced it down for about sixty-six miles in a direct line to the S. W. If I might hazard an opinion from appearance, to whatever part of the interior it leads, its source must be far to the N. E. or N. The capacity of its channel, and the terrific floods that must sometimes rage in it, would argue that it is influenced by tropical rains, which alone would cause such floods. It is likely that it seldom arrives at so reduced a state as that in which we found it, and that, generally speaking, it has a sufficient depth of water for the purposes of inland navigation : in such case its future importance cannot be questioned, since it most probably receives the chief streams falling westerly from the coast ranges. But, with every anticipation of the benefit that may at some time or other be derived from this remarkable and central stream, it is incumbent on me to state that the country, through which it flows, holds out but little prospect of advantage. Certainly the portion we

know of it, is far from encouraging.   The extent of alluvial
soil, between the inner and outer banks of the river, is extremely limited, and, instead of being covered with sward,
is in most places over-run by the polygonum.   Beyond this
the plains of the interior stretch away, whose character
and soil must change, ere they can be available to any
good purpose.   But there is a singular want of vegetable
decay in the interior of New Holland, and that powerfuily
argues its recent origin.

There is no life upon its surface, if I may so express myself; but the stillness of death reigns in its brushes,
and over its plains.   It cannot, however, be doubted that
we visited the interior during a most unfavorable season.
Probably in ordinary ones it wears a different appearance,
but its deserts are of great extent, and its productions are
of little value.

Agreeably to our arrangements, we broke up our camp at
an early hour on the morning of the 12th, and proceeded up
the river to the junction of New Year's Creek.   We then
struck away in an easterly direction from it, detaching a
man to trace the creek up, lest we should pass any water;
and we should certainly have been without it had we not
taken this precaution.

On the following day, we again passed to the eastward,
through an open country, having picturesque views of
Oxley's Table Land.   We crossed our track about noon,
and struck on the creek at about five miles beyond it, and
we were fortunate enough to procure both water and grass.

The timber upon the plains, between us and the Darling, we found to be a rough gum, but box prevailed in the neighbourhood of the creek at this part of it.

On the 14th, we changed our direction more to the southward, but made a short journey, in consequence of being obliged to make some slight repairs on the boat carriage.

On the 15th, we kept an E.S.E. course, and, crossing the creek at an early hour, got upon our old track, which we kept. We had the lateral ridge of the Pink Hills upon our right, and travelled through a good deal of brush. Four or five natives joined us, and two followed us to the end of our day's journey. In the course of the evening, they endeavoured to pilfer whatever was in their reach, but were detected putting a tin into a bush, and soon took to their heels. This was the first instance we had of open theft among the natives of the interior.

We passed Mosquito Brush on the 18th, but found the ponds quite dry, we were, therefore, under the necessity of pushing on, to shorten the next day's journey, as we could not expect to get water nearer than the marshes. At noon, on the 19th, we entered the plain, and once more saw them spreading in dreariness before us. While the party was crossing to the first channel, I rode to the left, in order to examine the appearance of the country in the direction of the wood, and as far as I skirted the reeds had my impressions confirmed as to their partial extension. I was obliged, however, to join the men without completing the

circuit of the marshes. They had found the first channel
dry, and had passed on to the other, in which, fortunately,
a small quantity of water still remained. It was, however,
so shallow as to expose the backs of the fish in it, and a
number of crows had congregated, and were pecking at
them. Wishing to satisfy my mind as to the distance to
which the river extended to the northward, Mr. Hume
rode with me on the following day, to examine the country
in that direction, leaving the men stationary. We found
that the reeds gradually decreased in body, until, at length,
they ceased, or gave place to bulrushes. There were general
appearances of inundation, and of the subsidence of waters,
but none that led us to suppose that any channel existed
beyond the flooded lands.

On our return to the camp, we observed dense masses of
smoke rising at the head of the marshes, and immediately
under Mount Foster. This excited our alarm for the
safety of the party we hoped to find at Mount Harris, and
obliged us to make forced marches, to relieve it if threatened by the natives.

On the 22d, we crossed the plains of the Macquarie, and
surprised a numerous tribe on the banks of the river; and the
difficulty we found in getting any of them to approach us,
their evident timidity, and the circumstance of one of them
having on a jacket, tended to increase our apprehensions.
When two or three came to us, they intimated that white
men either had been or were under Mount Harris, but we
were left in uncertainty and passed a most anxious night.

The body of reeds was still on fire; and the light embers were carried to an amazing distance by the wind, falling like a black-shower around us. As we knew that the natives never made such extensive conflagration, unless they had some mischievous object in view, our apprehension for the safety of Riley, with his supplies, was increased.

At the earliest dawn, we pushed for the hill. In passing that part of the meadows under Mount Foster, we observed that the grass had also been consumed, and we scarcely recognized the ground from its altered appearance. As we approached Mount Harris, we saw recent traces of cattle, but none were visible on the plains. Under the hill, however, we could distinctly see that a hut of some kind had been erected, and it is impossible for me to describe the relief we felt when a soldier came forward to reconnoitre us. I could no longer doubt the safety of the party, and this was confirmed by the rest of the men turning out to welcome us. It appeared that our suspicions with regard to the natives had not been without foundation, since they attempted to surprise the camp, and it was supposed the firing the marshes was done with a view to collect the distant tribes, to make a second attack; so that our arrival was most opportune.

The party I found awaiting our arrival at Mount Harris consisted of one soldier, Riley, who had the charge of the supplies, and a drayman. They had found the paper I had fixed against the tree, and also the letters I had hid, and had forwarded them to Sydney, by another soldier and a prisoner;

which had weakened their party a good deal. Riley informed me, that he had been between a month and three weeks at the station, and that knowing our provisions must have run short he had expected us much earlier than we had made our appearance.

My dispatches stated, that additional supplies had been forwarded for my use, together with horses and bullocks, in the event of my requiring them. On examination, the former were found to be in excellent order; and, as it would take some time to carry any changes I might contemplate, or find it necessary to make, into effect, I determined to give the men who had been with me a week's rest.

The camp was made snug; and as the weather had become much cooler, I thought it a good opportunity to slaughter one of the bullocks, in order to guard against any bad effects of our having been living for some weeks exclusively on salt provisions. I was also induced to this measure, from a wish to preserve my supplies as much as possible.

These matters having been arranged, I had a temporary awning erected near the river, and was for three or four days busily employed writing an account of our journey for the Governor's information.

Having closed my despatches, and answered the numerous friendly letters I had received, my attention was next turned to the changes that had taken place at Mount Harris during our absence. The Macquarie, I found, had wholly ceased to flow, and now consisted of a chain of ponds. Such of the minor vegetation as had escaped the fires of the natives, had perished under the extreme heat of the season. The acacia pendula stood leafless upon the plains, and the polygonum junceum appeared to be the only plant that had withstood the effects of the drought. Yet, notwithstanding this general depression of the vegetable kingdom, the animals that had been brought from Wellington Valley were in the best condition, and were, indeed, too fat for effective labour; it might, therefore, be reasonably presumed, that herbage affording such nourishment in so unfavourable a season, would be of the richest quality, if fresh and vigorous under the influence of seasonable, and not excessive, rains.

The appearance of the country was, however, truly melancholy; there was not a flower in bloom, nor a green object to be seen. Whether our arrival had increased their alarm, is uncertain, but the natives continued to fire the great marshes, and as the element raged amongst them, large bodies of smoke rose over the horizon like storm clouds, and had the effect of giving additional dreariness to the scene. I am inclined to think that they made these conflagrations to procure food, by seizing whatsoever might issue from the flames, as snakes, birds, or other animals; for they had taken every fish in the river, and the low state of its waters had enabled them to procure an abundance of muscles from its bed, which they had consumed with their characteristic improvidence. They were, consequently, in a starving condition, and so pitiable were their indications of it, that I

was induced to feed such of them as visited the camp, notwithstanding their late misconduct; being likewise anxious
to bring about a good understanding, as the best means of
ensuring the safety of the smaller party when we should
separate, of which I had reason to be doubtful. These
people had killed two white men not long before my arrival
among them, and as the circumstances attending the
slaughter are singular, I shall relate them.

The parties were two Irish runaways, who thought they
could make their way to Timor. They escaped from Wellington Valley with a fortnight's provision each, and a couple
of dogs, and proceeded down the Macquarie. About the
cataract, they fell in with the Mount Harris tribe, and remained with them for some days, when they determined on
pursuing their journey. The blacks, however, wanted to
get possession of their dogs, and a resistance on the part of
the Europeans brought on a quarrel. It appears, that before
the blacks proceeded to extremities, they furnished the Irish-
men, who were unarmed, with weapons, and then told them to
defend themselves, but whether against equal or inferior
numbers, I am uninformed. One of them soon fell, which
the other observing, he took his knife out, and cut the
throats of both the dogs before the blacks had time to put
him to death. He was, however, sacrificed; and both
the men were eaten by the tribe generally. I questioned several on the subject, but they preserved the most sullen si-
lence, neither acknowledging nor denying the fact.

Mr. Hume had been one day on Mount Harris, and while

there, had laid his compass on a large rock, near to which
Mr. Oxley's boat had been burnt. To his surprise, he found
the needle affected; and his bearings were all wrong. I
subsequently went up to ascertain the extent of the error
produced, and found it precisely the same as Mr. Hume
noticed. When I placed the compass on the rock, Mount
Foster bore from me N. by W., the true bearing of the
one hill from the other being N.N.W. My placing my note
book under the compass did not alter the effect, nor did the
card move until I raised the instrument a couple of feet
above the stone, when it first became violently agitated,
and then settled correctly; and my bearings of the highest
parts of Arbuthnot's Range, and of its centre, were as
follows:

Mount Exmouth to the N....... N. 86 E.
Centre .... N. 85 E.
Vernon's Peak .... N. 89 E.
                          Distance 70 miles.

Having finished my reports and letters, it became necessary
to consider the best point on which to move, and to fix a
day for our departure from Mount Harris. It struck me
that having found so important a feature as the Darling
River, the Governor would approve my endeavouring to
regain it more to the southward, in order to trace it
down. I, therefore, detached Mr. Hume to survey the
country in that direction, and to ascertain if a descent
upon the Bogen district would be practicable, through which
I had been informed a considerable river forced itself. The

report he made on his return was such as to deter me from that attempt, but he stated that the country for 30 miles from the Macquarie was well watered, and superior to any he had passed over during the journey; beyond that distance, it took up the character of the remote interior, and alternated with plains and brush, the soil being too sandy to retain water on its surface. He saw some hills from the extremity of his journey, bearing by compass W. S. W. We consequently determined to make for the Castlereagh, agreeably to our instructions. Preparations were made for breaking up the camp, all the various arrangements in the change of animals were completed, the boat carriage was exchanged for a dray, and I took Boyle in the place of Norman, whose timidity in the bush rendered him unfit for service.

There is a small hill on the opposite side of the river, and immediately facing Mount Harris, and to the S. E. of it there is a small lagoon, the head of a creek, by means of which its superfluous waters are carried off. This creek runs parallel to the river for about ten miles, and enters the marshes at the S. E. angle. This I ascertained one day in riding to carry on my survey of the southern extremity of the marshes, and to join my line of route by making the circuit of that part of them. I found that the river was turned to its northerly course by a rising ground of forest land, which checks its further progress westerly. I proceeded round the S. W. angle, and then, taking a northerly course, got down to the bottom of the first great marsh, thus com-

pleting the circuit of them. I did not return to the camp
until after 10 p. m., having crossed the river at day-light,
nor did we procure any water from the time we left the
stream to the moment of our recrossing it.

Having completed our various arrangements, and closed
our letters, we struck our tents on the morning of the 7th
March; we remained, however, to witness the departure of
Riley's party for Wellington Valley, and then left the Macquarie on an E. N. E. course for Wallis's Ponds, and made
them at about 14 miles.   They undoubtedly empty themselves into the marshes, and are a continuation of that
chain of ponds on which I left the party in Mr. Hume's
charge.   About a mile from Mount Harris, we passed a
small dry creek, that evidently lays the country under water
in the wet seasons.   There was a blue-gum flat to the eastward of it, which we crossed, and then entered a brush of
acacia pendula and box.   The soil upon the plain was an
alluvial deposit; that in the brushes was sandy.   From the
extremity of the plain, Mount Harris bore, by compass,
S.W. by W.; Mount Foster due west.   The scrub through
which we were penetrating, at length became so dense, that
we found it impossible to travel in a direct line through it,
and frequent ridges of cypresses growing closely together,
turned us repeatedly from our course.   The country at
length became clearer, and we travelled over an open forest
of box, casuarina, and cypresses, on a sandy soil; the first
predominating.   For about two miles before we made the
creek, the country was not heavily timbered, the acacia

pendula succeeding the larger trees. The ground had a good covering of grass upon it, and there were few of the salsolaceous plants, so abundant on the western plains, to be found. The rough-gum abounded near the creek, with a small tree bearing a hard round nut, and we had the luxury of plenty of water.

We remained stationary on the 8th, in hopes that Riley would have met the soldier who had been sent back to Wellington Valley, and that he would have forwarded any letters to us, of which he might have been the bearer. The day, however, passed over without realizing our expectations; and we started once more for the interior, and cut ourselves off from all communication with society.

We made for Morrisset's chain of ponds, and travelled over rich and extensive plains, divided by plantations of cypress, box, and casuarina, in the early and latter period of the day. About noon we entered a dense forest of cypresses, which continued for three miles, when the cypresses became mixed with casuarina, box, and mountain-gum, a tree we had not remarked before in so low a situation. We struck upon the creek after a journey of about 15 miles. It had a sandy bed, and was extremely tortuous in its course, nor was it until after a considerable search, that we at length succeeded in finding water, at which a party of natives were encamped. The moment they saw us, they fled, and left all their utensils, &c. behind them. Among other things, we found a number of bark troughs, filled with the gum of the mimosa, and vast quantities of gum made into cakes upon the ground. From this it would appear these unfortunate creatures were reduced to the last extremity, and, being unable to procure any other nourishment, had been obliged to collect this mucilaginous food.

The plains we traversed, were of uniform equality of surface. Water evidently lodges and continues on them long after a fall of rain, and in wet seasons they must, I should imagine, be full of quagmires, and almost impassable.

On the 10th, we passed through a country that differed in no material point from that already described. We stopped at 10 a. m. under some brush, in the centre of a large plain, from which Arbuthnot's range bore S. 84 E. distant from 50 to 55 miles, and afterwards traversed or rather crossed, those extensive tracts described by Mr. Evans as being under water and covered with reeds, in 1817. They now bore a very different appearance, being firm and dry. The soil was in general good, and covered with forest grass and a species of oxalia. We did not observe any reeds, or the signs of inundation, but, as is invariably the case with plains in the interior, they were of too even surface, as I have so lately remarked, to admit of the waters running quickly off them; and no doubt, when they became saturated, many quagmires are formed, that would very much impede the movements of an expedition.

We reached the Castlereagh about 4 p. m., and although its channel could not have been less than 130 yards in breadth, there was apparently not a drop of water in it. Its bed consisted of pure sand and reeds; amid the latter,

we found a small pond of 15 yards circumference, after a
long search. There is a considerable dip in the country towards the river, at about two miles from it; and the inter-
vening brush was full of kangaroos, which, I fancy, had congregated to a spot where there was abundance of food
for them. The soil covering the space was of the richest
quality, and the timber upon it consisted of box, mountain-
gum, and the angophora lanceolata, a tree that is never
found except on rich ground.

It appeared that our troubles were to recommence, and
that in order to continue on the Castlereagh, it would be
necessary for Mr. Hume and myself to undertake those
fatiguing journeys in search of water that had so exhausted
us already: and after all, it was doubtful how soon we might
be forced back. I had certainly expected that, on our
gaining the banks of the river, we should have had a constant supply of water, but the circumstance of the Castlereagh having not only ceased to flow, but being absolutely
dry, while it afforded the best and clearest proof of the severity and continuance of the drought in the interior, at
the same time damped the spirits and ardour of the men.
We kept the left bank of the river as we proceeded down
it, and passed two or three larger ponds about a mile
below where we had slept, but there they ceased. The
bed of the river became one of pure sand, nor did there
appear to be any chance of our finding any water in it.
I stopped the party at about eight miles, and desired the
men to get their dinners, to give Mr. Hume and myself time

to search for a supply upon the plains. Disappointed to
the left, we crossed the channel of the Castlereagh, and
struck over a small plain upon the right bank, and at the
extremity of it, came upon a swamp, from which we immediately returned for the cattle, and got them unloaded
by seven o'clock. As there was sufficient pasture around
us, I proposed to Mr. Hume on the following day, to leave
the party stationary, and to ride down the river to see how
far its present appearances continued. Like the generality
of rivers of the interior, it had, where we struck upon it, outer
banks to confine its waters during floods, and to prevent them
from spreading generally over the country; the space between the two banks being of the richest soil, and the
timber chiefly of the angophora kind. Flooded-gum overhung the inner banks of the river, or grew upon the many
islands, with casuarina. It became evident, however, that
the outer banks declined in height as we proceeded down the
river, nor was it long before they ceased altogether. As we
rode along, we found that the inner ones were fast decreasing in height also. Riding under a hanging wood of the
angophora, which had ceased for a time, we were induced
to break off to our right, to examine some large flooded-
gum trees about a couple of miles to the N. W. of us. On
arriving near them, we were astonished to find that they concealed a serpentine lagoon that had a belt of reeds round it.
Keeping this lagoon upon our right, we at length came to
the head of it, past which the river sweeps. Crossing the
channel of the river, we continued to ride in an easterly di-

rection to examine the country. In doing this, we struck
on a second branch of the Castlereagh, leading W. by N.
into a plain, which it of course inundates at times, and
running up it, we found its bed at the point of separation,
to be considerably higher than that of the main channel,
which still continued of pure sand — and was stamped all
over with the prints of the feet of natives, kangaroos, emus,
and wild dogs. We then turned again to the head of the lagoon, and took the following bearings of Arbuthnot's
range :

Mount Exmouth .... E. 30 S.
Centre Range .... E. 35 E.
Vernon's Peak .... E. 20 S.

From the head of the lagoon, the river appeared to enter
a reedy hollow, shaded by a long line of flooded-gum-trees;
and on proceeding to it, we found the banks ceased here altogether; and that a very considerable plain extended both
to the right and the left, which cannot fail of being frequently laid under water.

On the following morning we moved the party to the
lagoon, and, passing its head, encamped to the north of it;
after which we again rode down the river in search of
water. It continued to hold a straight and northerly course
for about five miles, having a plain on either side. The
reeds that had previously covered the channel then suddenly ceased, and the channel, contracting in breadth,
gained in depth: it became extremely serpentine, and at
length lost all the character and appearance of a river. It

had many back channels, as large as the main one, serving
to overflow the neighbouring country. We succeeded
in finding a small pond of water in one of the former,
hardly large enough to supply our necessities, but as it
enabled us to push so much further on, we turned
towards the lagoon, making a circuitous journey to the
right, across a large plain, bounded to the north by low
acacia brush and box. We struck upon a creek at the
further extremity of the plain, in which there was a tolerably sized pond. It appeared from the traces of men, that
some natives had been there the day before; but we did
not see any of them. The water was extremely muddy
and unfit for use. The lagoon at which we had em-
camped, was of less importance than we had imagined.

Whilst Mr. Hume led the party down the river, I rode
up its northward bank, to examine it more closely. I found
it to be a serpentine sheet of about three miles in length,
gradually decreasing in depth until it separated into two
small creeks. In following one of them up, I observed
that they re-united at the distance of about two miles, and
that the lagoon was filled from the eastward, and not by
the river as I had at first supposed. The waters at the
head of the lagoon were putrid, nor was there a fish in, or
a wild fowl upon it. The only bird we saw was a beautiful eagle, of the osprey kind, with plumage like a sea gull,
which had a nest in the tree over the tents.

In turning to overtake the party I rode through a great
deal of acacia scrub, and on arriving at the place at which

I expected to have overtaken them, I found they had pushed on.

The Castlereagh, as I rode down it, diminished in size considerably, and became quite choaked up with rushes and brambles. Rough-gum again made its appearance, with swamp-oak and a miserable acacia scrub outside. The country on both sides of the river seemed to be an interminable flat, and the soil of an inferior description.

I came up with Mr. Hume about 1 o'clock, and we again pushed forward at 3, and halted for the night without water, the want of which the cattle did not feel. The river held a general westerly course, and the country in its neighbourhood became extremely depressed and low. On the following day we moved forward a distance of not more than nine miles, through a country on which, at first, the acacia pendula alone was growing on a light alluvial soil. The river had many back drains, by means of which, in wet seasons, it inundates the adjacent plains. It was evident, however, that they had not been flooded for many years; and, notwithstanding that the country was low, the line of inundation did not appear to be very extensive, nor were there any reeds growing beyond the immediate banks of the river. Swamp-oak and rough-gum again prevailed near the stream at our halting place, and the improvement that had taken place, both in the country and in the Castlereagh, had induced us to make so short a journey; for not only was there abundance of the grass for the animals, but large ponds of water in the river. Some natives

had only just preceded us down it: we came upon their
fires that were still smoking; and upon them were the
remains of some fish they had taken, near which they
had left a cumbrous spear. The circumstances cheered us
with hopes that an improvement would take place in the
country, and that some new feature would soon open upon
us. In the course of the following day, however, every
favorable change, both in the river and in the country,
disappeared. The latter continued extremely depressed,
and in general open, or lightly covered with acacia pendula; the former dwindled into a mere ditch, choked up
with brambles and reeds, and having only here and there
a stagnant pool of water. We travelled on a N. W. ½ W.
course for about ten miles, and again stopped for the
night without water. In the course of the afternoon, we
traversed several flats, on which the rough-gum alone was
growing. These flats were evidently subject to flood;
and contained an alluvial soil.

They became more frequent as we travelled down the
river, and the work was so heavy for the animals, that I
was obliged to keep wide of them, in doing which we
struck upon a creek of large size, coming from the N. E.
and, having crossed, we traversed its right bank to its
junction with the Castlereagh, and stopped close to it at a
pond of water, though the feed for the animals was bad.
The country to the left of the river, though somewhat
high, was the same, in essential points, as that to the
right.

The Castlereagh seemed to have increased in size below the creek, but still it had no resemblance to a river. We had not proceeded very far down its banks, on the 18th, when we crossed a broad footpath leading to it from the interior. I turned my horse to the left, and struck upon a long sheet of water, from which I startled a number of pelicans. It was evident that the natives had recently been in the neighbourhood, but we thought it probable they might have been a hunting party, who had returned again to the plains. The whole track we passed over during the day was miserably poor and bare of vegetation, nor did the appearance of the country to the N.E. indicate any improvement. We lost the traces of the natives immediately after crossing their path or beat, and again found the bed of the river dry, after we had passed the sheet of water to which it led. The soil was so rotten and yielding, that the team knocked up early; indeed, it was a matter of surprise to me that they should not have failed before. The river made somewhat to the westward with little promise of improvement. The wretched appearance of the country as we penetrated into it, damped our spirits; we pressed on, however, with difficulty, over ground that was totally destitute of vegetation. Instead of lofty timber and a living stream, we wandered along the banks of an insignificant watercourse, and under trees of stunted size and scanty foliage. We stopped on the 20th at the angle of a creek, in which there was some dry grass, in consequence of the animals being almost in a starving state, but even here they had but little to eat·

A violent thunder-storm passed over us in the afternoon, but it made no change in the temperature of the air. The weather, although it had been hot and sultry, had fallen far short of the intense heat we experienced in crossing the marshes of the Macquarie, when it was such as to melt the sugar in the canisters, and to destroy all our dogs; and our nights were now become agreeably cool.

We still, however, continued to travel over a dead level, nor was a height or break visible from the loftiest trees we ascended. A little before we stopped at the creek, we surprised a party of natives; old men, women, and children. They were preparing dinners of fish in much larger quantities than they could have devoured — probably for a part of the tribe that were absent; but the moment they saw us they fled, and left every thing at our mercy. On examining the fish, we found them totally different from any in the Macquarie, and took two of the most perfect to preserve. In the afternoon one of the men came to inform me that the tribe was coming down upon us.

Mr. Hume and I, therefore, went to meet them. They were at this time about 150 yards from the tent, but seeing us advance, they stopped, and forming two deep, they marched to and fro, to a war song I suppose, crouching with their spears. We had not, however, any difficulty in communicating with them, and I shall detail the manner in which this was brought about, in hopes that it may help to guide others. When the natives saw us advance, they stopped, and we did the same. Mr. Hume then walked to a tree, and broke off a short branch. It is singular that this should, even with these rude people, be a token of peace. As soon as they saw the branch, the natives laid aside their spears, and two of them advanced about twenty paces in front of the rest, who sat down. Mr. Hume then went forward and sat down, when the two natives again advanced and seated themselves close to him.

Now it is evident that a little insight into the customs of every people is necessary to insure a kindly communication; this, joined with patience and kindness, will seldom fail with the natives of the interior. ·It is not to avoid alarming their natural timidity that a gradual approach is so necessary. They preserve the same ceremony among themselves. These men, who were eighteen in number, came with us to the tents, and received such presents as we had for them. They conducted themselves very quietly, and, after a short time, left us with every token of friendship.

On the 21st we proceeded down the river on a N.N.W. course, and at about five miles struck upon a very large creek, apparently coming from the E.N.E.

Although the Castlereagh had increased in size, this creek was infinitely larger; it was, however, perfectly dry. Lofty flooded-gum trees were upon its banks, and it appeared so much superior to the river that I was induced to halt the party at the junction, in order to examine it more closely. Mr. Hume, therefore, rode with me up the right bank. We had not proceeded very far, when some natives called out to us from the opposite scrub. Thinking that they belonged to the tribe we had left behind us, we pointed to the junction, and motioned them to go there, but one of the party continued to follow and call to us for some time. On our return to the men, we found that the natives had joined them, and they now gave us to understand that we were going away from water. This had indeed been apparent to us. The creek was perfectly dry, as far as we traced it up; and seemed to have been totally deserted by the natives.

We were about to proceed on our journey, when from twenty to thirty natives approached us from down the river. We sent two of those who had been with us to them, and the whole accompained us for some miles, talking incessantly to the men, but keeping at a very respectful distance from the animals. We at length got opposite to their camp, near which there was a very fine pool of water, and they were earnest in persuading us to stop at it. We were, however, too anxious to get forward to comply; under the improved appearance of the river since it had received the creeks from the eastward, little anticipating what was before us.

The natives did not follow us beyond their own encampment. Within sight of it, we came upon their armoury, if I may so term it. Numerous spears were reared against the trees, and heaps of boomerangs were lying on the ground. The spears were very heavy, and half barbed; and it is singular that three of them were marked with a broad arrow. We saw the natives watching us, fearful, I imagine, that we should help ourselves; but I would not permit any of their weapons to be touched.

Pursuing our journey, we reached another creek, at about five miles, similar to the last in appearance and size, and we crossed it repeatedly during the afternoon. We had been induced to keep along a native path in the hope that it would have led us to the river by a short cut; but it eventually led us to this creek, and away from the Castlereagh; for, notwithstanding that we subsequently changed our course to the S. W., we failed, as we supposed, again to strike upon the latter, and were obliged to stop for the night on the banks of what appeared to be a third large dry creek, which we intersected nearly at right angles.

We travelled through a good deal of brush during the day, nor did the country change from the miserable and barren character it had assumed for the last thirty or forty miles. The Castlereagh had so frequently changed, that both Mr. Hume and myself were puzzled as to the identity of the creek upon which we had halted. We searched its bed in vain for water, although it was most capacious. Under an impression that the river was still to the south, and that we were at a point to which many watercourses from the high lands tended, I crossed the creek early in the morning, and held a S. W. course, over an open forest country. At about eight miles, we came upon a large space over-run by the polygonum junceum, a certain indication of flooded ground, and of our consequent proximity to some stream. Accordingly, after pushing through it, we struck upon a small creek with abundance of water in it. Whether this creek was the Castlereagh, which it resembled much more than the one we had left in the morning, was doubtful; but it was a great source of comfort to us to have so unexpected a supply of water as that which was now at our disposal. Whatever channel this was, whether a river or a creek, our tracing it down would lead us in the direction we wished to go, and probably to some junction.

The neighbourhood of the creek was well clothed with vegetation, and the cattle found good feed; but the only trees near it were rough-gum and casuarinæ; the flooded-gum had again disappeared. The soil of the forest land over which we journeyed was a light sandy loam; and its timber consisted chiefly of eucalypti, acacia pendula, and the angophora.

Some natives visited us in the afternoon, and among them, both Mr. Hume and I recognized one of those we had seen on the Darling. He also knew us again, but we could not make out from him how far we were from that river. They staid with us till sunset, and then went down the creek, leaving their spears against a tree, for which they said they would return.

On the 23rd we took up a W.N.W. course, and when we again touched on the creek it was dry. This was at a distance of about five miles from where we had slept. As the animals had not recovered from their late privations, I deemed it better to halt the party and to examine the creek for a few miles below us, that in case it should prove des-

titute of water, we might return to that we had left. Mr.
Hume accordingly rode down it for about three miles, without success; and on his rejoining the men, we returned with
them to our last camp, or to within a short distance of it.
Wishing to examine the creek above our position, I requested
Mr. Hume to take two men with him, and to trace it down
in search of water, while I should proceed in the opposite
direction. I went from the camp at an early hour, and as
I wandered along the creek, I passed a regular chain of
ponds. The country on both sides of the creek was evidently subject to flood, but more extensively to the south
than to the north. From the creek, I struck away to my
left, and after penetrating through a belt of swamp-oak and
minor shrubs, got on a small plain, which I crossed N. E.
and, to my annoyance, found it covered with rhagodia and
salsolæ. As I had not started with the intention of sleeping, I turned to the S. W. a little before sunset, and reached
the tents betwen ten and eleven. I found Mr. Hume await_
ing me. He informed me that at about nine miles from
where we had turned back with the party, he had struck
upon a junction; and that as the junction was much larger
than the channel he had been tracing, he thought it better
to follow it up for a few miles. He found that it narrowed
in width, and that its banks became steep, with a fine avenue
of flooded-gum trees overhanging them. At four miles, he
came upon another junction, and at four miles more, found
himself opposite to the ground on which we had slept on the
previous Saturday. From this point he retraced the channel,

but not finding any water for three miles below the lower junction, he returned to the camp, with a view of prosecuting a longer journey on the morrow. Mr. Hume had become impressed with an opinion, that the junction up which we had slept was no other than the Castlereagh itself; and that our position was on a creek, probably Morrissett's chain of ponds, flowing into it. As the cattle wanted a few days' rest, Mr. Hume and I determined to ride, unattended, along our track to our camp of the 21st, and then to follow the channel upwards, until we should arrive at the station of the natives, or until we should have ridden to such a distance as would set our conjectures at rest. In the morning, however, instead of running upon our old track, we followed that of Mr. Hume to the junction, giving up our first intention, with a view to ascertain if there existed any water which we could, by an effort, gain, below where Mr. Hume had been. The channel was very broad, with a considerable fall in its bed, and, in appearance, more resembled the slope of a lawn than the bed of a river. It had two gum-trees in the centre of its channel, in one of which the floods had left the trunk of a large tree. We could discover where it narrowed and its banks rose, but, as we intended to make a closer examination before we left the neighbourhood, we continued our journey down the principal channel. The ground exhibited an abundance of pasture in its immediate neighbourhood, but the distant country was miserably poor and bare. At about three miles, we came upon the fresh traces of some natives, which led us to the channel again, from which we had wandered unintentionally. In it we found there had been water very lately, and it appeared that the natives had dug holes at the bottom to insure a longer supply. These were now exhausted, but still retained the appearance of moisture. At a mile and a half beyond these, we were led to some similar holes, by observing a number of birds flying about them. The water was too muddy for us to drink, but the horses emptied them successively. We now kept sufficiently near the channel to insure our seeing any pool that might still remain in it, but rode for about seven miles before we again saw water, and even here, although it was a spring, we were obliged to dig holes, and await their filling, before we could get sufficient for our use. Having dined, we again pursued our journey, and almost immediately came upon a long narrow ditch, full of water, and lined by bulrushes. The creek or river had for some time kept the centre of a deep alluvial valley, in which there was plenty of food for the cattle, and which, at this place, was apparently broader than anywhere else. The situation being favourable, we returned to the camp, and reached it late.

I do not know whether I was wrong in my conjecture, but I fancied, about this time, that the men generally were desponding. Whether it was that the constant fatigue entailed on myself and Mr. Hume, and that our constant absence, or the consequent exhaustion it produced, had any effect on their minds, or that they feared the result of our perseverance, is difficult to say ; but certainly, they all had a depression of spirits, and looked, I thought, altered in appearance; nor did they evince any satisfaction at our success—at least, not the satisfaction they would have shown at an earlier period of our journey.

Before moving forward, it remained for us to ascertain if the channel from the junction was the Castlereagh, or only a creek. The intersection of so many channels in this neighbourhood, most of them so much alike, made it essentially necessary that we should satisfy ourselves on this point. Mr. Hume, therefore, accompanied me, as had at first been intended the morning of our return to the place at which we had slept. We took fresh horses, but dispensed with any other attendants, and indeed went wholly unarmed.

After following our old track to its termination, we kept up the right bank of the channel, and at length arrived at the camp of the natives; thus satisfying ourselves that we had been journeying on the Castlereagh, and that we were still following it down. By this ride we ascertained that there was a distance of five-and-forty miles in its bed without a drop of water. Few of the natives were in the camp. The women avoided us, but not as if they were under any apprehension. Crossing at the head of the pool, we again got on our old track, but seeing two or three men coming towards us we alighted, and, tying our horses to a tree, went to meet them. One poor fellow had two ducks in his hand, which he had just taken off the fire; these he offered to us, and on our declining to accept of them, he called to a boy, who soon appeared with a large trough of honey, of which we partook. One of the men had an ulcer in the

arm, and asked me what he should do to heal it; indeed, I
believe Fraser had promised him some ointment, but not
having any with me, I signified to him that he should wash
it often, and stooping down, made as if I was taking up
water in my hand. The poor fellow mistook me, and, also
stooping down, took up a handful of dust which he threw
over the sore. This gave me the trouble of explaining
matters again, and by pointing to the water, I believe I at
length made him understand me.

These good natured people asked us where we had slept
the day we passed, and when informed of the direction,
shook their heads, motioning at the same time, that we
must have been without water. We informed them where
the party was, and asked them to come and see us, but I
fancy the distance was too great, or else we were in the
beat of another tribe. On mentioning these facts to the
men, they said that two of the natives had followed us for
some miles, calling out loudly to us, but Mr. Hume and I
both being in front, we did not hear them, although, evidently, they wished to save us distress.

Since the result of our excursion proved that the channel,
about which I had been so doubtful, was the Castlereagh,
it necessarily followed, that the creek at which we were encamped was one of those (most probably Morrisset's
chain of ponds,) which we had already crossed nearer its
source, and which Mr. Hume must have struck upon when
endeavouring to gain the Castlereagh from the marshes of
the Macquarie.

A perusal of these sheets will ere this have impressed on the reader's mind, the peculiarity of that fortune which led us from the Castlereagh to the creek, at which alone our wants could have been supplied. Had we wandered down the river, as we undoubtedly should have done had we recognised it as such, the loss of many of our animals would have been the inevitable consequence, and very probably a final issue would have been put to our journey. It is only to those who are placed in situations that baffle their own exertions or foresight, that the singular guidance of Providence becomes fully apparent.

It would appear that the natives were dying fast, not from any disease, but from the scarcity of food; and, should the drought continue, it seemed probable they may become extinct.

The men found the body of a woman covered with leaves near the tents, and very properly buried it. We made Friday a day of rest for ourselves, as indeed was necessary; and on the following morning proceeded down the river, and encamped on a high bank above it, at the base of which, our cattle both fed and watered.

At this spot one of the largest gum-trees I had ever seen had fallen, having died for want of moisture; indeed, the state of the vegetable kingdom was such as to threaten its total extinction, unless a change of seasons should take place.

It may be worthy of remark that, from our first arrival

on the banks of the Castlereagh, to our arrival at the
present camp, we never picked up a stone, or a pebble, in
its bed.

In the hope that we should fall on some detached pond,
we pursued our journey on the 29th. The Castlereagh
gave singular proofs of its violence, as if its waters, confined in the valley, had a difficuly in escaping from it. We
had not travelled two miles, when in crossing, as we imagined,
one of its bights, we found ourselves checked by a broad
river. A single glimpse of it was sufficient to tell us it was
the Darling. At a distance of more than ninety miles nearer
its source, this singular river still preserved its character,
so strikingly, that it was impossible not to have recognised
it in a moment. The same steep banks and lofty timber,
the same deep reaches, alive with fish, were here visible as
when we left it. A hope naturally arose to our minds, that
if it was unchanged in other respects, it might have lost
the saltness that rendered its waters unfit for use; but in
this we were disappointed—even its waters continued the
same. As it was impossible for us to cross the Darling, I
determined on falling back upon our last encampment,
which was at a most convenient distance, and of concerting
measures there for our future movements. Prior to doing
so, however, I rode to the junction of the Castlereagh with
the Darling, accompanied by Mr. Hume, a distance of
about half a mile. Upon the point formed by the two
streams, there were a number of huts, and on the opposite

bank of the Darling, about twenty natives had collected. We called out to them, but they would not join us.

At the junction, the Castlereagh, with whatever impetuosity it rushes from its confinement, makes not apparently the least impression on the Darling River. The latter seemed to roll on, totally heedless of such a tributary.

CHAPTER IV.

Perplexity — Trait of honesty in the natives — Excursion on horseback across the Darling — Forced to return — Desolating effects of the drought — Retreat towards the colony — Connection between the Macquarie and the Darling — Return up the banks of the Macquarie — Starving condition of the natives.

On our return to the party, we found them surrounded by the natives, who were looking with an eye of wonder on the cattle and horses. We pointed out to them the direction in which we were going, and invited them to visit us; and nothing appeared to astonish them so much as the management of the team by a single man. We got back to our position early, and again fixed ourselves upon it.

It now only remained for us to consider what we should do under circumstances of certainly more than ordinary perplexity. We had nothing to hope for from travelling in a southerly direction, while to the E. and N.E., the state of the country was worse than that by which we had penetrated to the Darling. It was evident, that the large creeks joining the Castlereagh in that direction were dry, since

the natives not only intimated this to us, but it was unquestionable that they themselves had deserted them, and
had crowded to such places as still contained a supply of
water.   Even in retreating, we could not hope to retrace
our steps.   Experience had proved to us, that the dry state
of the interior was as injurious to the movements of an
expedition as a too wet season would have been.   Taking
everything, therefore, into consideration, I determined on
leaving the party stationary, and on crossing the Darling
to the N.W., and, if any encouraging feature presented
itself, to return for the party, and persevere in an examination of the distant interior.   Such, at least, appeared to me
the most judicious plan : indeed, an attempt to have moved
in any other direction would have been fruitless.   And, as
the result of this journey would be decisive, and would
either fix or determine our advance or retreat, I was anxious for Mr. Hume's attendance.

The natives followed to the camp, and in the course of
the afternoon, were joined by their women.   The latter,
however, would not approach nearer than the top of a little
hillock on which they sat.   The men did not come round
the tents, but stood in a row at a short distance.   At
sunset, they gained a little courage, and wandered about a
little more; at length they went off to the Darling.

It was quite dark, when I heard a native call from the
hill on which the women had been, and I desired Hopkinson to take his firelock and ascertain what the man
wanted.   He soon after returned, and brought a blanket,

which he said the man had returned to him. The native was alone, and when he offered the blanket, kept his spear poised in his right hand; but, seeing that no violence was intended him, he lowered his weapon, and walked away.

I was extremely pleased at this trait of honesty, and determined to reward it. On inquiry, I found that the men had availed themselves of the day to wash their blankets, and that one of them had been flung over a bush hanging over the bank of the river, and it was supposed that one of the natives must have pulled it down with him. In the morning, the tribe went away from their encampment before day-light, as we judged from the cry of their dogs, than which nothing could be more melancholy; but about eight, the men made their appearance on the hill occupied by the women the evening previously, and seemed to be doubtful whether to approach nearer. I went out to them; and, with a downward motion of my hand, beckoned for them to come to me: they mistook the signal, but laid all their spears on the ground, and it was not until after the sign had been reversed that they stirred or moved towards us. I then got them in a row, and desired Hopkinson to single out the man who had given him the blanket. It was, however, with great difficulty that he recognised him, as the man stood firm and motionless. At length, after walking two or three times along the line, he stopped before one man, and put his hand on his shoulder, upon which the manner of the native testified as to the correctness of his guess.

The blanket being produced, I explained to the savage, with Mr. Hume's assistance, that I was highly pleased with him, and forthwith presented him with a tomahawk and a clasp-knife. The tribe were perfectly aware of the reason of my conduct, and all of them seemed highly delighted.

I was happy in having such an opportunity of shewing the natives of the interior that I came among them with a determination to maintain justice in my communication with them, and to impress them, at the same time, with a sense of our love of it in them. That they appreciated my apparent lenity in not calling for the defaulter, I am sure, and I feel perfectly conscious that I should have failed in my duty had I acted otherwise than I did.

Although the natives had shewn so good a disposition, as they were numerous, I thought it as well, since I was about to leave the camp, to shew them that I had a power they little dreamt of about me. I therefore called for my gun and fired a ball into a tree. The effect of the report upon the natives, was truly ridiculous. Some stood and stared at me, others fell down, and others ran away; and it was with some difficulty we collected them again. At last, however, we did so, and, leaving them to pick out the ball, mounted our horses and struck away for the Darling. We crossed the river a little above where we struck it, and then proceeded N. W. into the interior.

It is impossible for me to describe the nature of the country over which we passed, for the first eight miles.

We rode through brushes of polygonum, under rough-gum, without a blade of vegetation, the whole space being subject to inundation. We then got on small plains of firmer surface, and red soil, but these soon changed again for the former; and at 4 p. m. we found ourselves advanced about two miles on a plain that stretched away before us, and bounded the horizon. It was dismally brown; a few trees only served to mark the distance. Up one of the highest I sent Hopkinson, who reported that he could not see the end of it, and that all around looked blank and desolate. It is a singular fact, that during the whole day, we had not seen a drop of water or a blade of grass.

To have stopped where we were, would, therefore, have been impossible; to have advanced, would probably have been ruin. Had there been one favorable circumstance to have encouraged me with the hope of success, I would have proceeded. Had we picked up a stone as indicating our approach to high land, I would have gone on; or had there been a break in the level of the country, or even a change in the vegetation. But we had left all traces of the natives far behind us; and this seemed a desert they never entered — that not even a bird inhabited. I could not encourage a hope of success, and, therefore, gave up the point; not from want of means, but a conviction of the inutility of any further efforts. If there is any blame to be attached to the measure, it is I who am in fault, but none who had not like me traversed the interior at such a season, would believe the state of the country over which

I had wandered.   During the short interval I had been out, I had seen rivers cease to flow before me, and sheets of water disappear; and had it not been for a merciful Providence, should, ere reaching the Darling, have been overwhelmed by misfortune.

I am giving no false picture of the reality.   So long had the drought continued, that the vegetable kingdom was almost annihilated, and minor vegetation had disappeared.   In the creeks, weeds had grown and withered, and grown again; and young saplings were now rising in their beds, nourished by the moisture that still remained; but the largest forest trees were drooping, and many were dead.   The emus, with outstretched necks, gasping for breath, searched the channels of the rivers for water, in vain; and the native dog, so thin that it could hardly walk, seemed to implore some merciful hand to despatch it.   How the natives subsisted it was difficult to say, but there was no doubt of the scarcity of food among them.

We arrived in camp at a late hour, and having nothing to detain us longer, prepared for our retreat in the morning.   The natives had remained with the party during the greater part of the day, and had only left them a short time prior to our arrival.

When examining the creek on which we had been encamped for some days, Mr. Hume observed a small junction; and as we knew we were almost due N. of the marshes of the Macquarie, both of us were anxious to

ascertain whence it originated. To return to Mount Harris,
by retracing our steps up the Castlereagh, would have entailed the severest distress upon us; we the rather preferred proceeding up this creek, and taking our chance for a
supply of water. We therefore crossed Morrisett's chain of
ponds, and encamped in the angle formed by the junction
of the two creeks.

Before we left this position, we were visited by a party of
natives, twelve in number, but not of the Darling tribe.
They accompanied us a short way, and then struck off to
the right. At about a mile and a half, we crossed Mr.
Hume's track, leading westerly, which still remained observable. The creek was, no doubt, the hollow he stated
that he crossed on that excursion, and its appearance certainly justified his opinion of it. Its bed was choaked up
with bulrushes or the polygonum, and its banks were level
with the country on either side, or nearly so. We passed over
extremely rich soil the whole day, on a S. W. and by W.
course, though the timber upon it was dwarfish, and prin-
cipally of the rough-gum kind.

On the 2d of April, we stopped in order to make some
repairs upon the dray; the wheels of which had failed us.
Clayton put in four new spokes, and we heated the tyres
over again, by which means we got it once more serviceable.

The soil in the creek was of the richest quality, and was
found to produce a dwarf melon, having all the habits and
character of the cucumber. The fruit was not larger than a
pigeon's egg, but was extremely sweet. There were not,

however, many ripe, although the runners were covered
with flowers, and had an abundance of fruit upon them.
In the morning, we sent the tinker on horseback up the
creek, to ascertain how far the next water was from us,
desiring him to keep the creek upon his right, and to follow
his own track back again. He thought fit, however, considering himself a good bushman, to wander away to his left,
and the consequence was, that he soon lost himself. It
would appear that he doubled and passed through some
thick brush at the back of the camp, and at length found
himself at dark on the banks of a considerable creek. In
wandering along it, he luckily struck upon the natives we
had last seen, who, good-naturedly, led him to the track of
the dray, which his horse would not afterwards desert, and
the tinker sneaked into the tent about 3 o'clock in the
morning, having failed in his errand, and made himself the
butt of the whole party.

The day succeeding this adventure, we moved up the
creek, which was, for the most part, even with the plain.
The country continued the same as that we had passed
over from the junction, being subject to flood, and having
patches of bulrushes and reeds upon it. No change took
place in the timber, but the line of acacia pendula, which
forms the line of inundation, approached nearer to us; nor
was the mark of flood so high on the trunks of trees as below.
We halted, with abominable water, but excellent food for
the animals in the plains behind us. In continuing our
journey, we found several changes take place in the appear-

ance of the creek and its neighbourhood. The former diminished in size, and at length separated into two distinct channels, choaked up, for the most part, with dead bulrushes, but having a few green reeds in patches along it. The flats on either side became slightly timbered, and bluegum was the prevailing tree. Crossing one of the channels, we observed every appearance of our near approach to the marshes, the flats being intersected by many little water-runs, such as we had noticed at the bottom of them. About noon we struck upon a body of reeds under the wood of eucalypti, below the second great morass, and keeping a little to our right to avoid them, fell shortly afterwards into our old track on the plain, upon which we continued to move, making the best of our way to the channel which had supplied our wants on our first return from the Darling. It was now, however, quite dry, and we were obliged to push on further, to shorten the journey of the morrow.

The result of our journey up the creek was particularly satisfactory, both to myself and Mr. Hume; since it cleared up every doubt that might have existed regarding the actual termination of the Macquarie, and enabled us to connect the flow of waters at so interesting and particular a point. It will be seen by a reference to the chart, that the waters of the marshes, after trickling through the reeds, form a small creek, which carries off the superfluous part of them into Morrisett's chain of ponds, which latter again falls into the Castlereagh, at about eight miles to the W. N. W. and all three join the Darling in a W. by N. direction, in lat. 30°

52′ S. and E. lon. 147° 8′ at about 90 miles to the N. N. W.
of Mount Harris, and about an equal distance to the E. S. E.
of where we struck upon the last-mentioned river.   Thus it
is evident that the Darling had considerably neared the eastern ranges, although it was still more than 150 miles from
their base.   It was apparently coming from the N. E., and
whether it has its sources in the mountains behind our distant settlements, or still farther to the northwards, is a
question of curious speculation, although, as I have already
stated, I am of opinion that none but tropical rains could
supply the furious torrent that must sometimes rage in it.

It would be presumptuous to hazard any opinion as to the
nature of the interior to the westward of that remarkable
river.   Its course is involved in equal mystery, and it is a
matter of equal doubt whether it makes its way to the south
coast, or ultimately exhausts itself in feeding a succession
of swamps, or falls into a large reservoir in the centre of
the island.

We reached Mount Harris on the 7th of the month, and
moving leisurely up the banks of the Macquarie, gained Mr.
Palmer's first station on the 14th, and Wellington Valley on
the 21st, having been absent from that settlement four
months and two weeks.   The waters of the Macquarie had
diminished so much, that its bed was dry for more than half
a mile at a stretch, nor did we observe the least appearance
of a current in it, until after we had ascended the ranges.
The lower tribes were actually starving, and brought their
children to us to implore something to eat.   The men at-

tempted to surprise the camp, but I believe they were urged from absolute necessity to procure subsistence for themselves, and that they intended robbery rather than personal violence.

We left the interior in a still more deplorable state than that in which we found it; but it is more than probable, that under other circumstances, we should have found it impossible to traverse its distant plains, as it is certain that unless rain fell in less than three weeks, all communication with the Darling would have been cut off.

CHAPTER V.

General remarks — Result of the expedition — Previous anticipa-
tions — Mr. Oxley's remarks — Character ..of the Rivers flowing
westerly — Mr. Cunningham's remarks — Fall of the Macquarie —
Mr. Oxley's erroneous conclusions respecting the character of the
interior, naturally inferred from the state in which he found the
country — The marsh of the Macquarie merely a marsh of the
ordinary character — Captain King's observations — Course of the
Darling — Character of the low interior plain — The convict
Barber's report of rivers traversing the interior — Surveyor General
Mitchell's Report of his recent expedition.

WHETHER the discoveries that have been made during this
expedition, will ultimately prove of advantage to the colony
of New South Wales, is a question that time alone can
answer. We have in the meanwhile to regret that no beneficial consequences will immediately follow them. The further knowledge that has been gained of the interior is but
as a gleam of sunshine over an extensive landscape. A
stronger light has fallen upon the nearer ground, but the
distant horizon is still enveloped in clouds. The veil has only
as it were been withdrawn from the marshes of the Macquarie, to be spread over the channel of the Darling. Un-

satisfactory, however, as the discoveries may as yet be considered in a commercial point of view, the objects for which the expedition had been fitted out were happily attained. The marsh it had been directed to examine, was traversed on every side, and the rivers it had been ordered to trace, were followed down to their terminations to a distance far beyond where they had ceased to exist as living streams. To many who may cast their eyes over the accompanying chart, the extent of newly discovered country may appear trifling; but when they are told, that there is not a mile of that ground that was not traversed over and over again, either by Mr. Hume or by myself, that we wandered over upwards of 600 miles more than the main body of the expedition, on different occasions, in our constant and anxious search for water, and that we seldom dismounted from our horses, until long after sunset, they will acknowledge the difficulties with which we had to contend, and will make a generous allowance for them; for, however unsuccessful in some respects the expedition may have been, it accomplished as much, it is to be hoped, as under such trying circumstances could have been accomplished. It now only remains for me to sum up the result of my own observations, and to point out to the reader, how far the actual state of the interior, has been found to correspond with the opinions that were entertained of it.

I have already stated, in the introduction to this work, that the general impression on the minds of those best qualified to judge was, that the western streams discharged themselves

into a central shoal sea. Mr. Oxley thus expresses himself on the subject:—

" July 3d. Towards morning the storm abated, and at
day-light, we proceeded on our voyage. The main bed of
the river was much contracted, but very deep; the waters
spreading to the depth of a foot or eighteen inches over the
banks, but all running on the same point of bearing. We
met with considerable interruptions from fallen timber,
which in places nearly choaked up the channel. After
going about twenty miles, we lost the land and trees; the
channel of the river, which lay through reeds, and was from
one to three feet deep, ran northerly.—This continued for
three or four miles farther, when, although there had been
no previous change in the breadth, depth, or rapidity of the
stream for several miles, and I was sanguine in my expectations of soon entering the long-sought-for Australian sea,
it all at once eluded our farther pursuit, by spreading on
every point from N. W. to N. E. among the ocean of reeds
which surrounded us, still running with the same rapidity
as before. There was no channel whatever among those
reeds, and the depth varied from three to five feet. This
astonishing change (for I cannot call it a termination of the
river) of course left me no alternative but to endeavour to
return to some spot on which we could effect a landing before dark. I estimated, that during the day, we had gone
about twenty-four miles, on nearly the same point of bearing as yesterday. To assert, positively, that we were on
the margin of the lake, or sea, into which this great body

of water is discharged, might reasonably be deemed a conclusion, which has nothing but conjecture for its basis.
But if an opinion may be permitted to be hazarded from
actual appearances, mine is decidedly in favour of our being
in the immediate vicinity of an inland sea, or lake, most
probably a shoal one, and gradually filling up by numerous
depositions from the high lands, left by the waters which
flow into it. It is most singular, that the high lands on this
continent seem to be confined to the sea-coast, and not to
extend to any distance from it."

In a work published at Sydney, containing an account
of Mr. Allan Cunningham's journey towards Moreton Bay,
in 1828, the following remarks occur, from which it is
evident Mr. Cunningham entertained Mr. Oxley's views
of the character and nature of the Western interior. Towards the conclusion of the narrative, the author thus
observes:—

" Of the probable character of the distant unexplored interior, into which it has been ascertained *all* the rivers falling westerly from the dividing ranges flow, some inference
may be drawn from the following data.

" Viewing, between the parallels of 34° and 27°, a vast
area of depressed interior, subjected in seasons of prolonged
rains to partial inundation, by a dispersion of the several
waters that flow upon it from the eastern mountains whence
they originate; and bearing in mind at the same time, that the
declension of the country within the above parallels, as most
decidedly shewn by the dip of its several rivers, is uniformly

to the N. N. W. and N. W., it would appear very conclusive, that either a portion of our distant interior is occupied by a lake of considerable magnitude, or that the confluence of those large streams, the Macquarie, Castlereagh, Gwydir, and the Dumaresq, with the many minor interfluent waters, which doubtless takes place upon those low levels, forms one or more noble rivers, which may flow across the continent by an almost imperceptible declivity of country to the north or north-west coasts, on certain parts of which, recent surveys have discovered to us extensive openings, by which the largest accumulations of waters might escape to the sea."

It is the characteristic of the streams falling westerly from the eastern, or coast ranges, to maintain a breadth of channel and a rapidity of current more immediately near their sources, that ill accords with their diminished size, and the sluggish flow of their waters in the more depressed interior. In truth, neither the Macquarie nor the Castlereagh can strictly be considered as permanent rivers. The last particularly is nothing more than a mountain torrent. The Macquarie, although it at length ceased to run, kept up the appearance of a river to the very marshes; but the bed of the Castlereagh might have been crossed in many places without being noticed, nor did its channel contain so much water as was to be found on the neighbouring plains.

There are two circumstances upon which the magnitude, and velocity of a river, more immediately depend. The first is the abundance of its sources, the other the dip of its bed. If a stream has constant fountains at its head, and numerous tributaries joining it in its course, and flows withal through a country of gradual descent, such a stream will never fail; but if the supplies do not exceed the evaporation and absorption, to which every river is subject, if a river dependant on its head alone, falls rapidly into a level country, without receiving a single addition to its waters to assist the first impulse acquired in their descent, it must necessarily cease to flow at one point or other. Such is the case with the Lachlan, the Macquarie, the Castlereagh, and the Darling. Whence the latter originates, still remains to be ascertained; but most undoubtedly its sources have been influenced by the same drought that has ex.hausted the fountains of the three first mentioned streams.

In supporting his opinion of the probable discharge of the interior waters of Australia upon its north-west coast, Mr. Cunningham thus remarks in the publication from which I have already made an extract.

" To those remarkable parts of the north-west coast above referred to in the parallel of 16° south, the Macquarie river, which rises in lat. 33°, and under the meridian of 150° east, would have a course of 2045 statute miles throughout, while the elevation of its source, being 3500 feet above the level of the sea as shewn by the barometer, would give its waters an average descent of twenty inches to the mile, supposing the bed of the river to be an inclined plane.

" The Gwydir originating in elevated land, lying in 31° south, and long. 151° east, at a mean height of 3000 feet,

would have to flow 2020 miles, its elevated sources giving
to each a mean fall of seventeen inches.

" Dumaresq's river falling 2970 feet from granite mountains, in 28¼° under the meridian of 152°, would have to
pursue its course for 2969 miles, its average fall being
eighteen inches to a mile."

As I have never been upon the banks either of the Gwydir or the Dumaresq, I cannot speak of those two rivers;
but in estimating the sources of the Macquarie at 3500 feet
above the level of the sea, Mr. Cunningham has lost sight
of, or overlooked the fact, that the fall of its bed in the first
two hundred miles, is more than 2800 feet, since the cataract, which is midway between Wellington Valley and the
marshes, was ascertained by barometrical admeasurement,
to be 680 feet only above the ocean.   The country, therefore, through which the Macquarie would have to flow
during the remainder of its course of 1700 miles, in order to
gain the N.W. coast, would not be a gradually inclined plain,
but for the most part a dead level, and the fact of its failure
is a sufficient proof in itself how short the course of a river
so circumstanced must necessarily be.

Having conversed frequently with Mr. Oxley on the subject of his expeditions, I went into the interior preposessed
in favour of his opinions, nor do I think he could have
drawn any other conclusion than that which he did, from
his experience of the terminations of the rivers whose
courses he explored.   Had Mr. Oxley advanced forty, or
even thirty miles, farther than he did, to the westward of

Mount Harris; nay, had he proceeded eight miles in the
above direction beyond the actual spot from which he turned
back, he would have formed other and very different opinions of the probable character of the distant interior.   But
I am aware that Mr. Oxley performed all that enterprise,
and perseverance, and talent could have performed, and
that it would have been impracticable in him to have attempted to force its marshes in the state in which he found
them.   It was from his want of knowledge of their nature
and extent, that he inferred the swampy and inhospitable
character of the more remote country, a state in which subsequent investigation has found it not to be.   The marsh of
the Macquarie is nothing more than an ordinary marsh or
swamp in another country.   However large a space it covers,
it is no more than a concavity or basin for the reception of
the waters of the river itself, nor has it any influence whatever on the country to the westward of it, in respect to inundation; the general features of the latter being a regular alternation of plain and brush.   These facts are in themselves sufficient to give a fresh interest to the interior of
the Australian continent, and to increase its importance.

With respect to that part of its coast at which the rivers
falling from the eastern mountains, discharge themselves,
it is a question of very great doubt.   It seems that Capt.
King, in consequence of some peculiarities in the currents
at its N. W. angle, supports Mr. Cunningham's opinion as
to their probable discharge in that quarter.   But I fear the
internal structure of the continent is so low, as to preclude

the hopes of any river reaching from one extremity of it to
the other. . A variety of local circumstances, as the con-
traction of a channel, a shoal sea, or numerous islands, influence currents generally, but more especially round so
extensive a continent as that of which we are treating ; nor
does it strike me that any observations made by Capt. King
during his survey, can be held to bear any connection with
the eastern ranges, or their western waters. It may, how-
however, be said, that as the course of the Darling is still
involved in uncertainty, the question remains undecided ;
but it appears to me, the discovery of that river has set aside
every conjecture (founded on previous observation) respecting the main features of the interior lying to the westward
of the Blue Mountains. Both Mr. Oxley and Mr. Cunningham drew their conclusions from the appearances of
the country they severally explored. The ground on which
those theories were built, has been travelled over; and has
not been found to realize them, but subsequent investigation
has discovered to us a river, the dip of whose bed is to the
S.W. We have every reason to believe that the sources of
this river must be far to the northward of the most distant
northerly point to which any survey has been made, as we
are certain that it is far beyond the stretch of vision from
the loftiest and most westerly of the barrier ranges ; from
which circumstance, it is evident that whatever disposition
the streams descending from those ranges to the westward
may shew to hold a N.W. course more immediately at the
base, the whole of the interior streams, from the Macquarie

to the Dumaresq, are tributaries to the principal channel which conveys their united waters at right angles, if not still more opposite to the direction they were supposed to take, as far as is yet known.

The Darling River must be considered as the boundary line to all inland discoveries from the eastward. Any judgment or opinion of the interior to the westward of that stream, would be extremely premature and uncertain. There is not a single feature over it to guide or to strengthen either the one or the other.

My impression, when travelling the country to the west and N. W. of the marshes of the Macquarie, was, that I was traversing a country of comparatively recent formation. The sandy nature of its soil, the great want of vegetable decay, the salsolaceous character of its plants, the appearance of its isolated hills and flooded tracts, and its trifling elevations above the sea, severally contributed to strengthen these impressions on my mind. My knowledge of the interior is, however, too limited to justify me in any conclusion with regard to the central parts of Australia. An ample field is open to enterprise and to ambition, and it is to be hoped that some more decisive measures will be carried into effect, both for the sake of the colony and of geography, to fill up the blank upon the face of the chart of Australia, and remove from us the reproach of indifference and inaction.

Since the above pages were written, an expedition was undertaken by Major Mitchell, the Surveyor-General, to ascertain the truth of a report brought in by a runaway convict of the name of Barber, or Clarke, who had been at large for five years, at different times, among the natives to the northward of Port Macquarie. This man stated that a large river, originating in the high lands near Liverpool Plains, and the mountains to the north of them, pursued a N. W. course to the sea. His story ran thus: Having learnt from the natives the existence of this river, he determined to follow it down, in hopes that he might ultimately be enabled to make his escape from the colony. He accordingly started from Liverpool Plains, and kept on a river called the Gnamoi, for some time, which took him N. W. After a few days' journey, he left this river, traversed the country northwards, and crossed some lofty ranges. Descending to the N. E. he came to another large river, the Keindur, which again took him N. W. He travelled 400 miles down it, when he observed a large stream joining it upon its left bank, which he supposed to be the Gnamoi. The river he was upon was broad and navigable. It flowed through a level country with a dead current and muddy water, and spread into frequent lakes. He found that it ultimately discharged itself into the sea, but was uncertain at what distance from its sources. He was positive he never travelled to the *southward of west*. He ascended a hill near the sea, and observed an island in the distance, from which, the natives informed him, a race of light-coloured men came in large canoes for a scented wood; but having failed in the immediate object of his journey, he was eventually obliged to return.

The following official report of Major Mitchell will sufficiently point out the incorrectness of the preceding statement. It is most probable that Barber merely told that which
he had heard from the natives, and that having a more than
ordinary share of cunning, he made up a story upon their
vague and uncertain accounts, in hopes that it would benefit him, as in truth it did.

––––––

> " *Bullabalakit, on the River Nammoy,*
> *in lat.* 30° 38′ 21″ *S., long.* 149° 30′ 20″ *E.*
> 23d *December,* 1831.

"Sir,

"I have the honour to state, for the information of His
Excellency the Governor, the progress I have made in
exploring the course of the interior waters to the northward
of the Colony, with reference to the letter which I had the
honour to address to Col. Lindesay, on this subject, on the
19th ult.

"On crossing Liverpool Range my object was to proceed
northward, so as to avoid the plains and head the streams
which water them, and avoiding also the mountain ranges
on the east.

"I arrived accordingly, by a tolerably straight and level
line, at Walamoul, on Peel's River; this place (a cattle
station of Mr. Brown) being nearly due north from the
common pass across Liverpool Range, and about a mile-

and-a-half above the spot where Mr. Oxley crossed this river.

"I found the general course of the Peel below Wala-moul to be nearly west; and after tracing this river down-wards twenty-two miles (in direct distance), I crossed it at an excellent ford, named Wallamburra. I then traversed the extensive plain of Mulluba; and leaving that of Coonil on the right, extending far to the north-east, we passed through a favourable interval of what I considered Hard-wicke's Range, the general direction of this range being two points west of north.

"On passing through this gorge, which, from the name of a hill on the south side, may be named Ydire, I crossed a very extensive tract of flat country, on which the wood consisted of iron-bark and acacia pendula; this tract being part of a valley evidently declining to the north-west, which is bounded on the south by the Liverpool Range, and on the south-west by the extremities from the same. On the west, at a distance of twenty-two miles from Hard-wicke's Range, there stands a remarkable isolated hill named Bounalla; and towards the lowest part of the coun-try, and in the direction in which all the waters tend, there is a rocky peak named Tangulda. On the north, a low range (named Wowa), branching westerly from Hard-wicke's Range, bounds on that side this extensive basin, which includes Liverpool Plains. Peel's River is the principal stream, and receives, in its course, all the waters of these plains below the junction of Connadilly,—which I take to be York's River, of Oxley.

" The stream is well known to the natives by the name Nammoy; and six miles below Tangulda, the low extremities from the surrounding ranges close on the river, and separate this extensive vale from the unexplored country which extends beyond to an horizon which is unbroken between W. N. W. and N. N. W.

" The impracticable appearance of the mountains to the northward, induced me to proceed thus far to the west; and on examining the country thirty miles N.E. by N. from Tangulda, I ascended a lofty range extending westward from the coast chain, and on which the perpendicular sides of masses of trachyte (a volcanic rock) were opposed to my further progress even with horses : it was therefore evident that the river supposed to rise about the latitude of 28° would not be accessible, or at least available to the Colony, in that direction, and that in the event of the discovery of a river beyond that range flowing to the northern or north-western shores, it would become of importance to ascertain whether it was joined by the Nammoy, the head of this river being so accessible that I have brought my heavily laden drays to where it is navigable for boats, my present encampment being on its banks six miles below Tangulda. From this station I can perceive the western termination of the Trachytic range, and I am now about to explore the country between it and the Nammoy, and the further course of this river; and in the event of its continuance in a favourable direction, I shall fix my depôt on its right bank, whence I now write, and descend the stream in the portable boats.

    " I have the honour to be, Sir,

      " Your most obedient servant,

        " T. L. MITCHELL,

         " *Surveyor-General.*"

" *The Hon. The Colonial Secretary.*"

      " *Peel's River, 29th February,* 1832.

 " SIR,

 " I have the honour to inform you, for the information of His Excellency the Governor, that I have reached the left bank of this River with my whole party on my return from the northern interior, having explored the course of the river referred to in my letter of 22d December last, and others within the 29th parallel of latitude.

 " There was so much fallen timber in the Nammoy, and its waters were so low, that the portable boats could not be used on that river with advantage, and I proceeded by land in a north-west direction, until convinced by its course turning more to the westward that this river joined the river Darling. I therefore quitted its banks with the intention of exploring the country further northward, by moving round the western extremities of the mountains mentioned in my former letter, and which I have since distinguished

in my map by the name of the Lindesay Range. These
mountains terminate abruptly on the west, and I entered a
fine open country at their base, from whence plains (or rather open ground of gentle undulation) extended westward
as far as could be seen. On turning these mountains I
directed my course northward, and to the eastward of north,
into the country beyond them, in search of the river *Kin-
dur;* and I reached a river flowing westward, the bed of
which was deep, broad, and permanent, but in which there
was not then much water.

" The marks of inundation on trees, and on the adjoin-
ing high ground, proved that its floods rose to an extraor-
dinary height; and from the latitude, and also from the
general direction of its course, I considered this to be the
river which Mr. Cunningham named the Gwydir, on crossing it sixty miles higher, on his route to Moreton Bay. I
descended this river, and explored the country on its left
bank for about eighty miles to the westward, when I found
that its general course was somewhat to the southward of
west. This river received no addition from the mountains
over that part of its left bank traversed by me ; and the heat
being intense, the stream was at length so reduced that I
could step across it. The banks had become low, and the
bed much contracted, being no longer gravelly, but muddy.
I therefore crossed this river and travelled northward, on a
meridian line, until, in the latitude of 29° 2', I came upon
the largest river I had yet seen. The banks were earthy
and broken, the soil being loose, and the water of a white

muddy colour. Trees, washed out by the roots from the soft soil, filled the bed of this river in many places. There was abundance of cod-fish of a small size, as well as of the two other kinds of fish which we had caught in the Peel, the Nammoy, and the Gwydir. The name of this river, as well as we could make it out from the natives, was Karaula. Having made fast one tree to the top of another tall tree, I obtained a view of the horizon, which appeared perfectly level, and I was in hopes that we had at length found a river which would flow to the northward and avoid the Darling. I accordingly ordered the boat to be put together, and sent Mr. White with a party some miles down to clear away any trees in the way. Mr. White came upon a rocky fall, and found besides the channel so much obstructed by trees, and the course so tortuous, that I determined to ascertain before embarking upon it, whether the general course was in the desired direction. Leaving Mr. White with half the party, I accordingly traced the Karaula downwards, and found that its course changed to south, a few miles below where I had made it, and that it was joined by the Gwydir only eight miles below where I had crossed that river. Immediately below the junction of the Gwydir (which is in latitude 29° 30′ 27″, longitude 148° 13′ 20″) the course of the river continues southward of west, directly towards where Captain Sturt discovered the River Darling; and I could no longer doubt that this was the same river. · I therefore returned to the party, determined to explore the country further northward.

" The results of my progress thus far were sufficient, I considered, to prove that the division of the waters falling towards the northern and southern shores of Australia is not, as has been supposed, in the direction of the Liverpool and Warrabangle range, but extends between Cape Byron on the eastern shore, towards Dick Hartog's Island on the west; the greater elongation of this country being between these points, and intermediate between the lines of its northern and southern coasts. The basin of the streams I have been upon must be bounded on the north by this dividing ground or water-shed, and although no rise was perceptible in the northern horizon, the river was traversed by several rocky dykes, over which it fell southward; their direction being oblique to the course, and nearly parallel to this division of the waters. I beg leave to state, that I should not feel certain on this point without having seen more, were it not evident from Mr. Cunningham's observations, made on crossing this division on his way to Moreton Bay. Mr. Cunningham, on crossing the head of this river, nearly in the same latitude, but much nearer its sources, found the height of its bed above the sea to be 840 feet; at about forty-five miles further northward the ground rose to upwards of 1700 feet, but immediately beyond, he reached a river flowing north-west, the height of which was only 1400 feet above the sea. He had thus crossed this dividing higher ground, between the parallels of 29° and 28°. It appears, therefore, that all the interior rivers we know of to the northward of the Morum-

bidgee, belong to the basin of the Karaula; this stream
flowing southward, and hence the disappearance of the
Macquarie and other lower rivers may be understood, for
all along the banks of the Karaula, the Gwydir, and the
Nammoy, the country, though not swampy, bears marks of
frequent inundation; thus the floods occasioned by these
rivers united, cover the low country, and receive the Macquarie, so that no channel marks its further course.

" That a basin may be found to the northward receiving
the waters of the northern part of the coast range in a
similar manner is extremely probable, and that they form a
better river, because the angle is more acute between the
high ground, which must bound it on the N.E. and the
watershed on the south.   I therefore prepared to cross the
Karaula, in hopes of seeing the head at least of such a
river, and to explore the country two degrees further
northward, but moving in a N.W. direction.   My tent was
struck, and I had just launched my portable boat for the
purpose of crossing the river, when Mr. Surveyor Finch,
whom I had instructed to bring up a supply of flour,
arrived with the distressing intelligence, that two of his
men had been killed by the natives, who had taken the
flour, and were in possession of everything he had brought
— all the cattle, including his horse, being also dispersed
or lost.   I therefore determined not to extend my excursion
further, as the party were already on reduced rations, and
on the 8th instant I retired from the Karaula, returning by
the marked line, which being cut through thick scrubs in

various places, is now open, forming a tolerably direct line
of communication in a N.W. direction from Sydney, to a
river, beyond which the survey may be extended whenever
His Excellency the Governor thinks fit.

" The natives had never troubled my party on our advance; indeed I only saw them when I came upon them
by surprise, and then they always ran off.   Their first visit
was received at my camp on the Karaula, during my absence down that river, when they were very friendly, but
much disposed to steal.   Various tribes followed us on
coming back, but never with any shew of hostility, although moving in tribes of a hundred or more parallel to
our marked line, or in our rear; it was necessary to be ever
on our guard, and to encamp in strong positions only,
arranging the drays for defence during the night: three
men were always under arms, and I have much pleasure in
stating, that throughout the whole excursion, and under
circumstances of hardship and privation, the conduct of
the men was very good.   I took an armed party to the
scene of pillage, and buried the bodies of the two men,
who appeared to have been treacherously murdered while
asleep by the blacks during the absence of Mr. Finch:
no natives were to be found when I visited the spot,
although it appeared from columns of smoke on hills which
overlooked it, that they were watching our movements.

" The party has now arrived within a day's journey of
Brown's station, and I have instructed Assistant-Surveyor
White (from whom I have received great assistance during

the whole journey) to conduct it homewards, being desirous to proceed without delay to Sydney, and to receive the instructions of His Excellency the Governor.

    " I have the honour to be, Sir,

        " Your most obedient Servant,

            " T. L. MITCHELL,

                " Surveyor-General."

" The Hon. The Colonial Secretary,

    " &c. &c. &c."

CHAPTER VI.

CONCLUDING REMARKS.

Obstacles that attend travelling into the interior of Australia — Diffi_
culty of carrying supplies —Importance of steady and intelligent subordinates — Danger from the natives — Number of men
requisite — And of cattle and carriages — Provisions — Other arrangements — Treatment of the natives — Dimensions of the boat
used in our second expedition.

HAVING now had considerable experience in the fitting
out and management of expeditions in New South Wales,
I cannot refrain from making some few observations on the
subject. And without presuming to lay down any fixed
rules, I shall only refer to those by which I have best succeeded, in hopes that some of my remarks may prove of
use to future travellers who may venture to penetrate
into the trackless deserts over so small a portion of which
I wandered.

The great difficulty of examining the interior of Australia, is that of carrying supplies; for increasing the number
of individuals composing an expedition is of no avail,
since an additional number of men must necessarily in-

crease the consumption of food.   In order to meet this difficulty it has been proposed to establish depôts, upon which an expedition could fall back to recruit its supplies, and in ordinary cases this plan might answer; but I am decidedly of opinion that no party could long remain stationary in the distant interior without some fatal collision with the natives, which would be attended with the most deplorable consequences; and I do think, considering all things, that the experiment is too dangerous to be tried; for when I reached Mount Harris, on my first retreat from the Darling, I found the party who were awaiting me, with a supply of provisions, under very great alarm, in consequence of the hostile proceedings of the Mount Harris tribe.   The men had been obliged to put the camp into a state of defence. The blacks had attempted to surprise them, and would, had I not returned, have combined in some general attack. It appears to me that the most judicious plan would be to send a supply of provisions, with an expedition, to a distant point, under the charge of a minor party.   These provisions could replace those already expended, and the animals that carried them could be taken back.

The number of individuals of which the expedition down the banks of the Macquarie was composed, was fourteen : that is to say, myself, Mr. Hume, two soldiers, one free man, and seven prisoners of the crown.   The latter behaved, on all occasions, as steadily as it was possible for men to do.   Yet the circumstance of the two soldiers being with me increased my confidence in the whole, for I was aware that their example would influence the rest. However well disposed the prisoners of the crown may be, (as in this instance they certainly were,) the beneficial example of steady discipline cannot be denied. I should not have considered myself justified in leaving the camp as I did for a week, and in detaching Mr. Hume at the same time when at the bottom of the marshes, or in making the last effort to maintain our position on the banks of the Darling, if I had not reposed every confidence in the man to whom I entrusted the safety of the camp during my absence.

Experience, therefore, of the value of the two soldiers, whom General Darling was good enough to permit me to take on the strength of the party, fully bears me out in recommending that one man, at least, of general responsibility shall be attached to all future expeditions. The success of an expedition depends so much on the conduct of the persons of whom it is composed, that too much attention cannot be given to the selection even of the most subordinate. Men of active intelligent minds, of persevering habits, and of even temper, should be preferred to mechanics who do not possess these most requisite qualities. On the other hand, it is impossible to do without a good carpenter, however defective he may be in other respects. I was indebted to Mr. Maxwell, the superintendant of Wellington Valley, for some excellent men, both on my first and on my second journey, because he understood the nature of the service for which they were required, and the

characters of those whom he recommended.   But however
well selected the party, or the men rather, might be, I still
consider a man of general responsibility necessary for its
complete organization.   I would have him somewhat superior to the rest in his station in life.   Him I would hold an-
swerable for the immediate discipline of the camp, whilst I
was present, and for its safety when absent.   The assistant
to the leader I would put entirely out of the question.   He
has other and most important duties to perform.   I would
rate this man wholly independent of him.

In reference to what I have already said with regard to
the natives, it was supposed that they were so little to be
apprehended, that when I went on the first occasion into
the interior, I applied for a limited number of men only,
under an impression that with a few men I could carry provisions equal to a consumption of a greater number, and by
this means be enabled to keep the field for a greater length of
time.   But I do not think it would be safe to penetrate into
the distant country with fewer than fifteen men, for although, happily, no rupture has as yet taken place with the
natives, yet, there is no security against their treachery,
and it is very certain that a slight cause might involve an
expedition in inextricable difficulty, and oblige the leader
to throw himself on the defensive, when far away from other
resources than those with which he should have provided
himself, and that, perhaps, when navigating a close and
intricate river, with all the dangers and perplexities attendant on such a situation.   It is absolutely necessary to

establish nightly guards, not only for the security of the camp, but of the cattle, and at the same time to have a force strong enough to maintain an obstinate resistance against any number of savages, where no mercy is to be expected. It will be borne in mind, that there is a wide difference between penetrating into a country in the midst of its population, and landing from ships for the purpose of communication or traffic. Yet, how few voyages of discovery have terminated without bloodshed! Boats while landing are covered by their ships, and have succour within view; but not so parties that go into unknown tracts. They must depend on their immediate resources and individual courage alone.

With regard to the animals, I should recommend an equal number of horses as of bullocks; since it has been found that the latter, though slow, travel better over swampy ground than horses, which, on the other hand, are preferable for expeditious journeys, to which bullocks would never be equal. One of the colonial pack-saddles weighs fifty pounds complete, and is preferable to those sent out from England. This, with a load of 250 lbs. is sufficient for any animal, since it enables the men to place a part of their provisions with the general loads. The difficulty of keeping the backs of the animals free from injury, more especially where any blemish has before existed, is exceedingly great. They should undergo an examination twice a-day, that is, in the morning prior to moving off, and in the afternoon before they are turned out to feed; and measures should then be taken to ease them as circumstances require. I never suffered the saddles to be removed from the backs of the animals under my charge for twenty minutes after the termination of the journey for the day, in order to guard against the effects of the sun; and where the least swelling appeared the saddle was altered and the place dressed. Yet, notwithstanding all this care and attention, several both of the horses and bullocks were at one time in a sad condition, during the first journey,—so much so as almost to paralize our efforts. It would be advisable. that such animals as are entirely free from blemish should be chosen for the service of expeditions, for, with proper management they might be kept in order. The anxiety of mind attendant on a bad state of the animals is really quite embarrassing, for it not only causes a delay in the movements, but a derangement in the loads. Other animals are overburdened, and there is no knowing where the evil will stop.

In addition to the pack-animals, I would recommend the employment of a dray or cart under any practicable circumstances. It serves to carry necessary comforts, gives an expedition greater facility for securing its collections, and is of inconceivable advantage in many other respects.

Constant and most earnest attention should be paid to the issue of provisions, on the discreet management of which so much depends, and the charge of them should be committed to the second in command. The most important articles are flour, tea, sugar, and tobacco. All should be husbanded with extreme care, and weighed from time to

time. The flour is best carried in canvass bags, containing
100 pounds each, and should at the termination of each
day's journey, be regularly piled up and covered with a
tarpauline.   Tea, sugar, and tobacco lose considerably in
weight, so that it is necessary to estimate for somewhat
more than the bare supply.   With regard to the salt meat,
the best mode of conveying it appears to be in small barrels
of equal weight with the bags of flour.   Salt pork is better
than beef.   It should be deprived of all bones and be of the
very best quality.   I have heard spirits recommended, but
I do not approve their use.   Tea is much more relished by
the men; indeed they could not do well without it. A small
quantity of spirits would, however, of course be necessary
in the event of its being required.

Mr. Cornelius O'Brien, an enterprising and long-estab-
lished settler, who has pushed his flocks and herds to the
banks of the Morumbidgee, was good enough to present
me with eight wethers as I passed his station.   It may be
some gratification to Mr. O'Brien to know, that they
contributed very materially to our comforts, and he will,
perhaps, accept my acknowledgements in this place, not
only for so liberal a present to myself, but for his attention
and kindness to my men as long as they remained in his
neighbourhood.   It was found that the sheep gave but little
additional trouble, requiring only to be penned at night,
as much to secure them from the native dogs as to prevent
them from straying away.   They followed the other animals
very quietly, and soon became accustomed to daily move-

ments. They proved a most available stock; no waste attended their slaughter, and they admitted of a necessary and wholesome change of fresh food from the general salt diet, on which the men would otherwise have had to subsist.

The provisions should, if possible, be issued weekly, and their diminution should be so regulated as to give an equal relief to the animals.

For general information I have annexed a list of the supplies I took with me on my first expedition. It may appear long, but the articles were packed in a small compass, and their value immaterial.

As a precautionary measure I should advise, that one of the pack animals be kept apart for the purpose of carrying water. Two casks of equal weight are the best for such a purpose. In long and hot marches, the men experience great relief from having water at hand.

In reference to the natives, I hope sufficient has been said of the manner of communicating with them to prevent the necessity of a repetition here. The great point is not to alarm their natural timidity: to exercise patience in your intercourse with them; to treat them kindly; and to watch them with suspicion, especially at night. Never permit the men to steal away from the camp, but keep them as compact as possible; and at every station so arrange your drays and provisions that they may serve as a defence in case of your being attacked.

The natives appeared to me to be indifferent to our presents, in most cases. Tomahawks, knives, pieces of iron, and different coloured ribbons for the forehead, were most esteemed by them. They will barter and exchange their fish for articles, and readily acquire confidence.

I believe I have now touched on all the more important points : on minor ones no observation I can make will be of use; men must, in many things, be guided by circumstances.

———

I may here notice that, in my second expedition, as it was anticipated that I should require adequate provision for water conveyance, at one stage or other of my journey down the Morumbidgee, I was furnished with a whale-boat, the dimensions of which are given below. She was built by Mr. Egan, the master builder of the dock-yard and a native of the colony, and did great credit to his judgment. She carried two tons and a half of provisions, independently of a locker, which I appropriated for the security of the arms, occupying the space between the after-seat and the stern. She was in the first instance put together loosely, her planks and timbers marked, and her ring bolts, &c. fitted. She was then taken to pieces, carefully packed up, and thus conveyed in plank into the interior, to a distance of four hundred and forty miles, without injury. She was admirably adapted for the service, and rose as well as could have been expected over the seas in the lake. It was evident, however, that she would have been much safer if she had

had another plank, for she was undoubtedly too low. The following were her dimensions:—

Breadth across 7th timber aft, 5 ft. $\frac{1}{2}$ an inch outside.

Across 12th timber, 5 ft. 11$\frac{1}{4}$ in.

Across 17th timber forward, 5 ft.

25 ft. 8 in. in length inside.

Curve of the keel No. 1, from the after side of each apron, 3 ft. 3$\frac{3}{4}$ in.

No. 2, from head to head of the dead wood, 13$\frac{1}{2}$ in.

No. 3, from one end of keel to the other inner side, 3 in.

No. 4, round of keel from the toe of each dead wood, $\frac{1}{2}$ $\frac{1}{16}$th.

The timbers were marked, beginning from the stern to the bow on the starboard side, and from bow to stern on the larboard.

APPENDIX.

No. I.

LETTER OF INSTRUCTIONS.

By His Excellency Lieutenant General Ralph Darling, Commanding His Majesty's Forces, Captain-General and Governor-in-Chief of the Territory of New South Wales, and its dependencies, and Vice Admiral of the same, &c. &c. &c.

To Charles Sturt, Esq. Captain in the 39th Regiment of Foot.

WHEREAS it has been judged expedient to fit out an expedition for the purpose of exploring the interior of New Holland, and the present dry season affords a reasonable prospect of an opportunity of ascertaining the nature and extent of the large marsh or marshes which stopped the progress of the late John Oxley Esq, Surveyor General, in following the courses of the rivers Lachlan and Macquarie in the years 1817 and 1818. And whereas I repose full confidence in your abilities and zeal for conducting such an expedition, I do hereby constitute and appoint you to command and take charge of the expedition now preparing for the purpose of exploring the interior of the country, and for ascertaining, if practicable, the nature and extent of the marsh or marshes above mentioned.

In the prosecution of this service, you will be guided generally by the following instructions.

1. You will be accompanied on this expedition by Mr. Hamilton Hume, whose great experience in travelling through the remote parts of the Colony, cannot fail to be highly useful to you. You will also be attended by two soldiers and six convicts, of whom one is to understand the shoeing of horses, one to be a carpenter, one a harness-maker, and three stockmen, and you will be provided with six horses and twelve bullocks.

2. A small boat has been built here for the use of the expedition, and for its conveyance, there is provided a light four-wheeled carriage to be drawn by two bullocks.

    The deputy Commissary General has received orders for supplying the expedition with provisions of the best quality sufficient for six months' consumption, together with tents, blankets, clothing, pack-saddles, utensils, instruments, tools, and necessaries of all kinds of which you are likely to stand in need. Orders are also given for providing you with arms and ammunition, with rockets for signals, and an ample supply of simple medicines — You are to consider it an important dut to attend to the providing of all these supplies, and to take care that not only every article is of the best quality that can be procured, but also that no article be wanting with which you may desire to be provided.

3. Orders are given for forwarding without delay all your provisions, stores and supplies of every kind to Wellington Valley, at which place, you, Mr. Hume, and all your men

are to rendezvous as soon as possible. Mr. Maxwell, the superintendant, will furnish you with well-trained bullocks, and afford you all the assistance you may require in arranging every thing for your departure from that station.

4. After you shall have completed all your arrangements, you are to lose no time in finally departing from Wellington Valley in prosecution of the immediate objects of the expedition.

5. You are first to proceed to Mount Harris, where you are to form a temporary depot, by means of which you will have an opportunity of more readily communicating with Mr. Maxwell.

6. You are then to endeavour to determine the fate of the Macquarie River, by tracing it as far as possible beyond the point to which Mr. Oxley went, and by pushing westward, you are to ascertain if there be any high lands in that direction, or if the country be, as it is supposed, an unbroken level and under water. If you should fail in those objects, you will traverse the plains lying behind our north-west boundaries, with a view to skirt any waters by which you may have been checked to the westward; and if you should succeed in skirting them, you are to explore the country westward and southward as far as possible, endeavouring to discover the Macquarie beyond the marsh of Mr. Oxley, and following it to its mouth if at all practicable.

7. There is some reason to believe that the over-flowing of the Macquarie when visited by Mr. Oxley, was occasioned by heavy rains falling in the mountains to the eastward, and that as you are to visit the same spot at a different season of the year, you may escape such embarrassment; but although you should get beyond the point at which

Mr. Oxley stopped, it would not be prudent to risk your own health or that of your men, by continuing long in a swampy country. Therefore it may be advisable for you in the first instance to leave the greater part of your men, bullocks, and baggage, at Mount Harris, and if you should see a probability of your being able to cross into the interior, you will then return to Mount Harris for such additional supplies as you may judge necessary. You can there communicate with Mr. Maxwell respecting any ulterior arrangements which you may be desirous of making.

8. The success of the expedition is so desirable an object, that I cannot too strongly impress upon you the importance of perseverance in endeavouring to skirt any waters or marshes which may check your course as long as you have provisions sufficient for your return; but you must be cautious not to proceed a single day's journey further than where you find that your provisions will be barely sufficient to enable you to reach the nearest place at which you can depend upon getting supplies.

9. If after every endeavour you should find it totally impracable to get to the westward, you are still to proceed northward, keeping as westerly a direction as possible; and when the state of your provisions will oblige you to retreat, you will be guided by your latitude, as to the place to which you are to make the best of your way, but you are not to make for any place on the coast, if Wellington valley should still be nearer.

10. You must be aware that the success of the expedition will greatly depend upon the time for which your provisions

will hold out, and therefore you will see the great importance of observing every possible economy in the expenditure of provisions, and preventing waste of every kind.

11. You are to keep a detailed account of your proceedings in
a journal, in which all observations and occurrences of every
kind, with all their circumstances, however minute, are to be
carefully noted down. You are to be particular in describing the general face of all the country through which you
pass, the direction and shape of the mountains, whether
detached or in ranges, together with the bearings and estimated distances of the several mountains, hills, or eminences
from each other. You are likewise to note the nature of
the climate, as to heat, cold, moisture, winds, rains, &c, and
to keep a register of the temperature from Fahrenheit's thermometer, as observed at two or three periods of each day.
The rivers, with their several branches, their direction, is
velocity, breadth, and depth, are carefully to be noted. It
further expected that you will, as far as may be in your
power, attend to the animal, vegetable, and mineral productions of the country, noting down every thing that may
occur to you, and preserving specimens as far as your
means will admit, especially some of all the ripe seeds
which you may discover; when the preservation of specimens is impossible, drawings or detailed accounts of them,
are very desirable.

12. You will note the description of the several people whom
you may meet, the extent of the population, their means
of subsistence, their genius and disposition, the nature of
their amusements, their diseases and remedies, their objects

of worship, religious ceremonies, and a vocabulary of their language.

Lastly. On your return from your journey, you are to cause all the journals or other written documents belonging to, and curiosities collected by the several individuals composing the expedition, to be carefully sealed up with your own seal and kept in that state until you shall have made your report to me in writing of the result of the expedition.

Given at Sydney, this eighteenth day of November, 1828.

By Command of His Excellency the Governor,

ALEXANDER M'LEAY.

No. II.

LIST OF STORES SUPPLIED FOR THE EXPEDITION.

List of Articles delivered from His Majesty's Stores, in charge of D. A. C. Goodsir, to Captain Sturt, viz.—

1 Hack saddle.
1 Bridle.
2 Tents.
14 Pack saddles.
14 Pair hobbles.
24 Sets horse shoes.
2000 Horse nails.
113 Fathoms 1½ inch rope.
1 Hammer, (Blacksmith's)
1 Paring knife.
2 Chipping do.
2 Rasps.
1 Pair pincers.
1 Cutter.
2lb. Pack thread.
24 Needles.
¼lb. Bristles.
7lbs. Leather.
½lb. Thread.

9 Harness casks.
23 Canvas bags.
4 Tin cases.
16 Padlocks.
6 Tarpaulens.
10 Havresacks.
113 Fathom one-inch rope.
1 Boat compass.
1 Telescope.
1 Spare glass for ditto.
1 Tin case (for charts.)
100 Fish-hooks, (large.)
12 Fishing-lines.
10 Knives.
10 Forks.
10 Spoons.
2 Frying-pans.
2 Tinder-boxes.
1 Tea-kettle, (tin.)

1 Pair of steelyards.

10 Tin pots.

1 Flour seive.

2 Felling-axes.

4 Tomahawks.

2 Hammers.

1 Hand-saw.

3 Bill-hooks.

3 Awls.

3 Broad hoes.

4 Razors.

4 Brushes.

4 Combs.

3 Iron pots, (camp kettles.)

1 Pair scissars.

10 Tin dishes.

8 Jackets.

8 Duck frocks.

8 Shirts.

16 Trowsers.

24 Pair shoes.

16 Blankets.

16 Pair stockings.

2 Bullock collars.

2 Do. back-bands and pipes.

2 Leading cruppers.

1 Boat with sail and oars.

1 Do. carriage.

1 Canvass boat-cover.

3 Water breaker.

Commissariat Office, Sydney, Nov. 10th, 1828.

P. S.—1 Tarpaulen.

Large Fish-hook.

1 Tin tea-kettle.

1 Camp kettle.

Pitch and oil.

Hemp or twine.

No. III.

SHEEP — FARMING RETURNS, SHEWING THE INCREASE IN FOUR YEARS, *from two Breeding Flocks, consisting of* 670 *Ewes in Lamb.*

(A.)— 1st JUNE, 1828.

Flocks.	Breeding Ewes.		Lambs.		Total.	Remarks.	
	2 yrs. old.	3 yrs. old.	Male.	Female.			Lambs.
No. 1	330		148	149	627	Deaths 6. Increase	297
— 2		330	154	154	638	4 Do.	308
				•	1265	10	605

ABSTRACT.

Purchased two Flocks of Ewes, at 84s................... 670 Ewes.
Increase of Lambs 605
   Casual Deaths 10 596

    Total as per Return......................... 1265

(B.)— 1st JUNE, 1829.

Flocks.	Breeding Ewes.	Maiden Ewes.	Wethers.	Rams.	Lambs.		Total.	Remarks.	
					Male.	Female			Lambs.
No. 1 3-yr.	327				154	154	635	Deaths 3. Increase	308
2 4-yr.	326				155	155	636	Do. 4 ,,	310
3 1-yr.		302					302	Do. 1 ,,	618
4 1-yr.			302	18			320	,, 8	
							1893		

ABSTRACT.

Return (A) Total.................................... 1265
Increase by Lambing 618
Ditto Rams purchased 18
        — 636
   Casual Deaths 8 628

    Total as per Return 1893

* The increase throughout these returns is calculated at from 270 to 290 Lambs, to 300 Ewes, which is the usual average in N. S. W.

(C.)—1st JUNE, 1830.

Flocks.	Breeding Ewes.	Maiden Ewes.	Wethers.	Rams.	Lambs.		Total.	Remarks.
					Male.	Female		Lambs.
No.								
1 2-yr.	296				133	133	562	Deaths 6. Incr. 266
2 4-yr.	325				150	150	625	,, 2 Ditto 300
3 5-yr.	326				160	160	646	Ditto 390
4 2-yr.			302	27			329	
5 1-yr.			309				309	886
6 1-yr.		309					309	
								3 Rams died
							2780	12 ditto purchased.

ABSTRACT.

Return (B) Total.. 1893
Increase by Lambing 886
Ditto Rams purchased 12
————896

Deaths................................ 11 887

Total as per Return........... 2780

(D.)—1st JUNE, 1831.

Flocks.	Breeding Ewes.	Maiden Ewes.	Wethers.	Rams.	Lambs.		Total.	Remarks.
					Male.	Female		Lambs.
No.								
1 2-yr.	304				136	136	576	Deaths 5 Incr. 272
2 3-yr.	293				135	136	564	Do. 3 Do. 271
3 5-yr.	324				156	156	636	Do. 1 Do. 312
4 6-yr.	320				156	156	632	Do. 2 Do. 312
								Killed 4
5 3-yr.			300				300	Deaths 2
6 2-yr.			308				308	Ditto 1
7 1-yr.			443				443	
8 1-yr.		442					442	Ditto 1
9				40			40	Ditto 5
							3941	20
								Purchased 12

Lambs 1167

ABSTRACT.

Return (C) Total.................................... 2780
Increased by Lambing....................1167
Ditto Rams purchased...................... 18
————1185

Casual deaths 20.—Killed for use 4........ 24 1161

————
3941

(E.)—1st JUNE, 1832.

Flocks.	Breeding Ewes.	Maiden Ewes.	Wethers.	Rams.	Lambs.		Total.	Remarks.
					Male.	Female		
No.								Lambs.
1 2-yr.	344				154	154	652	Dths. 6 Incr. 308
2 3-yr.	344				162	161	667	Do. 4 Do. 323
4 3-yr.	342				164	165	671	Do. 3 Do. 329
5 6-yr.	320				155	155	630	Do. 2 Killed 2 310
6 7-yr.	300				145	145	590	Do. 2 Do. 18 290
7 4-yr.			300				300	1560
8 3-yr.			302				302	Do. 2
9 2-yr.			440				440	Do. 1 Killed 2
10 1-yr.			583				583	22
11 1-yr.		584					584	
12				45			45	Do. 5 Purchd. 10
								25 Casual deaths
	1650	584	1625	45	780	780	5464	

ABSTRACT.

Return (D) Total 3941
Increase by Lambing 1560
Do. by purchase of Rams 10
           —— 1570
    Decrease by casual death......... 25
    Do. by slaughtered for use......... 22   1523
            —— 47 ——
       Grand Total............. 5464   as above.

Memorandum,—The deaths have been calculated at the lowest rate under the best management. It may be safer to assume a rate of four or five per cent. per annum.

Account of Expenditure and Income upon Sheep Stock in Australia, appended to Returns A. B. C. D. & E.

1st YEAR, (RETURN A.) JUNE, 1829.

INCOME.

By 1265 fleeces, average weight 2¼lbs. 2846lbs. wool at 1s. 6d. per lb. £213 9 0

EXPENDITURE.

	£					
To 2 Shepherds at £30	£ 60	0	0			
To 1 Watchman 20	20	0	0	PROFIT.		
To Hurdles, &c.	10	0	0			
	90	0	0			
				£123	9	0

2nd YEAR, (B.) JUNE, 1830.

INCOME.

By 1893 fleeces, at 2¼lbs. 4259lbs. wool at 1s. 6d. £319 8 6

EXPENDITURE.

	£					
To 2 Shepherds at £30	£ 60	0	0			
To 2 Ditto 20	40	0	0			
To 1 Watchman	20	0	0			
To Hurdles &c.	5	0	0			
	£125	0	0			
To 18 Rams at £10*	180	0	0			
	£305	0	0	14	8	6

3rd YEAR, (C.) JUNE, 1831.

INCOME.

By 2780 fleeces, at 2¼lbs. 6255lbs. wool at 1s. 6d. £469 2 6

EXPENDITURE.

	£					
To 2 Shepherds at £30	£ 60	0	0			
To 1 Ditto 25	25	0	0			
To 3 Ditto 20	60	0	0			
To 2 Watchmen 20	40	0	0			
To Hurdles, &c.	10	0	0			
	195	0	0			
To 12 Rams at £10.	120	0	0			
	£315	0	0	154	2	6

Carried forward.......... £292 0 0

* The price of Rams will probably fall to £5.

PROFIT.

Brought forward...... £292 0 0

4th YEAR, (D.) JUNE, 1832.

INCOME.

By 3941 fleeces, at 2¼lbs. 8867lbs. wool at
1s. 6d............................ £665 0 0.

EXPENDITURE.

To 2 Shepherds at £30	£ 60 0 0	
To 2 Ditto 25	50 0 0	
To 4 Ditto 20	80 0 0	
To 3 Watchmen, &c. (1 to take charge of Rams)	80 0 0	
To Hurdles, &c.	10 0 0	
	260 0 0	
To 18 Rams at £10.	180 0 0	
		£440 0 0
		225 0 0

5th YEAR, (E.) JUNE, 1833.*

INCOME.

By 5464 fleeces at 2¼lbs 12,294lbs. wool at
1s. 6d............................ £922 0 0

EXPENDITURE.

To 2 Shepherds at £30	£ 60 0 0	
To 3 Ditto 25	75 0 0	
To 5 Ditto 20	100 0 0	
To 3 Watchmen 20	60 0 0	
To Hurdles, &c.	20 0 0	
	315 0 0	
To 10 Rams at £10.	100 0 0	
		£415 0 0
		507 0 0

Nett Profit by sales of Wool, in five years...... £1024 0 0

£1024 divided by 5, gives £204 8s. 0d. for annual interest, on the original
capital of £2814, (about 7¼ per cent. per annum,) in addition to the accumulation of capital itself, shewn by the valuation of stock.

* These accounts are a year in advance of the Sheep returns, in order to bring
them to the time at which the wool would be sold.

VALUATION OF SHEEP, JUNE, 1832.---(RETURN E.)

1614 Ewes from 1 to 4 years old £3 each..................	£4842	0	0
620 Do. 4 to 7 years old 2 ,, ...	1240	0	0
780 Female Lambs.......... 2 ,, ...	1560	0	0
2405 Wethers and Male Lambs 15s.	1803	0	0
45 Rams (original cost, 450l.)	400	0	0
	£9845	0	0

Note.—About £500 would be added to the Income on the fifth year, by the sale of Wethers of 3 and 4 years old.

The cost of Rams ought, strictly speaking, to be added to capital, and not deducted from Income ; but these returns were made out in their present form at the request of a gentleman proceeding to the Colony with a limited capital, and who wished to know how much he might safely invest in sheep.

No. IV.

LIST OF GEOLOGICAL SPECIMENS, COLLECTED IN THE DISTANT INTERIOR DURING THE FIRST EXPEDITION, WITH THEIR LOCALITIES AND THEIR RELATIVE DISTANCES FROM EACH OTHER.

It may be necessary to observe that the height of the Cataract of the Macquarie River above the sea, was ascertained by barometrical admeasurement to be 650 feet. The country subsequently traversed is considerably lower. The specimens refer only to the geological formation of the distant interior.

Schorl Rock.—Colour blueish grey, fine grained, extremely hard. Composed of Tourmaline and Quartz. Forms the bed of the Macquarie at the Cataract, 75 miles to the N. W. of Wellington Valley.

Decomposed Mica Slate.—Colour white; yields to the knife; adheres strongly to the tongue.

Decomposed Feldspar.—Colour pale rose-pink; very fine grained; easily scratched with the knife; adheres strongly to the tongue.

Both specimens immediately succeed the Schorl rock at the Cataract, in large smooth-sided masses.

This formation may be said to terminate the rocks connected with the dividing ranges, since it is the last that occurs at their western base.

A little below the Cataract, the county undergoes a remarkable change, and becomes extremely depressed.

Porphyry with Feldspar.—Colour dull red, with white spots, or grey with red spots; very hard, compact, sonorous, magnetic. [See pp. 27 and 115.] Composition of Mount Harris, a hill called by Mr. Oxley, elevated about 170 feet above the level of the plains. It lies 53 miles to the N. N. W. of the Cataract, and is about 16 miles distant from the first of the marshes of the Macquarie.

Porphyry with Feldspar.—Colour grey with red spots, similar to the last. Was not observed to affect the needle. Formation of Mount Foster. Mount Foster is more than 200 feet in height, and lies about 5 miles to the N. N. W. of Mount Harris. From the summit of both, Arbuthnot's range is visible, bearing nearly due east, distant 70 miles. [See page 28.]

Quartz Rock varieties—Slaty Quartz varieties. —Composition of the first elevations to the Westward of the marshes of the Macquarie, called New Year's Range, a group of five hills. The loftiest about 200 feet in elevation; distant about 80 miles to the N. W. of Mount Harris.

Granite.—Colour red, coarse-grained. Composed of Quartz, Feldspar, and Mica.

Granite, Porphyritic.—Colour light red. Both occur in the bed of New Year's Creek, traversing it obliquely, and are visible for a

A SELENITE.

CHRYSTALLIZED SULPHATE OF LIME.

Published by Smith,Elder & C.º Cornhill,London.

few hundred yards only. This granite occurs about 16 miles from the Range in a N. by E. direction.

Old Red Sandstone.—Composition of Oxley's Table Land, 500 feet above the level of the plains. It is broken into two hills, that appear to have been separated by some convulsion. [See page 81.] It bears N. W. by W. from New Year's Range, distant 50 miles.

Old Red Sandstone,—Composition of D'Urban's group. The highest elevation ascended during the expedition, being nearly 600 feet above the level of the plain in which it rises. It lies to the S. S. W. of Oxley's Table Land, distant 40 miles, and the rock of which it is composed is much harder and closer.

Breccia.—Colour pale yellow, silicious cement. Composition of some trifling elevations to the North of New-Year's range, with which it is doubtful whether they are connected.

Chrystallized Sulphate of Lime.— Found imbedded in the alluvial soil forming the banks of the Darling river. Occurring in a regular vein. Soft, yielding to the nail; not acted on by acids.—See Plate.

Breccia.—Pale ochre colour, silicious cement, extremely hard. Cellular, and sharp edges to the fractured pebbles. Has apparently undergone fusion. Occurs in the bed of the Darling in one place only.

Sandstone Varieties.—Colour dull red and muddy white; appears like burnt bricks; light, easily frangible; adheres to the tongue; occurs in large masses in the bed of the Darling;

probably in connection with the rock-salt of the neighbourhood, which, from the number of brine springs discovered
feeding the river, must necessarily exist.

Variety of the same description of rock.

Jasper and Quartz.—Shewing itself above the surface of a plain,
from which D'Urban's group bore S. 40 E. distant 33 miles.

It is a remarkable fact, that not a pebble or a stone was picked up during the progress of the expedition, on any one of the
plains ; and that after it again left Mount Harris for the Castlereagh, the only rock-formation discovered was a small Free-
stone tract near the Darling river.   There was not a pebble of
any kind either in the bed of the Castlereagh, or in the creeks falling into it.

No. V.

OFFICIAL REPORTS TO THE COLONIAL GOVERNMENT.

GOVERNMENT ORDER.

Colonial Secretary's Office, 23d January, 1829.

His Excellency the Governor has been pleased to order, that the following communication, dated the 25th of December last, from Captain Sturt, of the 39th Regiment, who is employed in an exploring expedition into the interior of the country, be published for general information.

By his Excellency's Command,

ALEXANDER M‘LEAY.

Western Marshes, 25th December, 1828.

Sir,—I do myself the honor to forward, for the Governor's perusal, a copy of my journal up to the date of my

arrival at Mount Harris. I should not have directed the
messenger to return so soon, had I not subsequently advanced to Mount Foster, and surveyed the country from
that eminence. I could distinctly see Arbuthnot's Range
to the eastward. From that point the horizon appeared to
me unbroken, but the country to the northward and westward seemed to favour an attempt to penetrate into it. I
did not observe any sheet of water, and the course of the
Macquarie was lost in the woodlands below.

Mr. Hume ascended the hill at sun-rise, and thought he
could see mountains to the north east, but at such a distance as to make it quite a matter of uncertainty. Agree-
ing, however, in the prudence of an immediate descent, we
left our encampment on the morning of the 23d, under
Mount Foster, to which we had removed from Mount Harris, and pursued a north-north-west course to the spot on
which we rest at present. We passed some fine meadow
land near the river, and were obliged to keep wide of it in
consequence of fissures in the ground. Traversing a large
and blasted plain, on which the sun's rays fell with intense
heat, and on which there was but little vegetation, we
skirted the first great morass, and made the river immediately beyond it. It is of very considerable extent, the channel of the river passing through it. We are encompassed
on every side by high reeds, which exist in the woods as
well as in the plains. Mr. Hume and myself rode forward
yesterday through the second morass, and made the river
on slightly elevated ground, at a distance of about five
miles; the country beyond appeared to favour our object,
and we, to-morrow, proceed with the party to the north-
west. The river seems to bend to the north-east; but in

this level country it is impossible to speak with certainty, or to give any decided opinion of the nature of it, beyond the flats on which we are travelling. The reeds to the north-east and northward extend over a circumference of fifty miles; but if Mr. Hume really saw mountains or rising ground in the former point, the apparent course of the Macquarie is at once accounted for. The country, however, seems to dip to the north, though generally speaking it is level, and I am inclined to think that the state of the atmosphere caused a deception in this appearance.

I regret to add, that the effects of the sun on the plain over which we passed on the 23d produced a return of inflammation in the eyes of the men, I have named in my journals, and caused the same in the eyes of several others of my party. I halted, therefore, to expedite their recovery. They are doing well now, and we can proceed in the cool of the morning without any fear of their receiving injury by it. One of the men, who were to return to Wellington Valley, was attacked slightly with dysentery, but the medicines I gave him carried it off in the course of a day or two. I have taken every precaution with regard to the health of the men, in preparing them for the country into which they are going; and I have to request that you will inform the governor that the conduct of the whole party merits my approbation, and that I have no fault to find. The men from Sydney are not so sharp as those from Wellington Valley, but are equally well disposed. The animals, both horses and bullocks, are in good order, and I find the two soldiers of infinite service to me. The boat has received some damage from exposure to intense heat, but is otherwise uninjured. We still retain the carriage, and have every prospect of dragging it on with us.

His Excellency, having been good enough to order a fresh supply of provisions to Wellington Valley, I have to beg they may be forwarded to Mount Harris, and that the person in charge thereof be instructed to remain at that station for one month. We shall, during the interval, have examined the country to the north-west; and, in case we are forced back, shall require a supply to enable us to proceed to the northward, in furtherance of the views I have already had the honor to submit for the Governor's approval.

I have the honor to be, Sir,

Your most obedient and humble Servant,

CHARLES STURT,

Captain, 39th Regt.

The Honourable the Colonial Secretary.

GOVERNMENT ORDER.

Colonial Secretary's Office, 6th April, 1829.

His Excellency the Governor is pleased to direct that the following interesting Report which has been received from Captain Sturt, 39th Regiment, who has been employed for some months past, (as will be seen on reference to the Government Order, No. 4, published with Captain Sturt's First Report in the Sydney Gazette, of the 24th of January last) in exploring the interior, be communicated for the information of the public.

It appears that the river Macquarie ceases to exist near the spot where the expedition under the late Mr. Oxley terminated, which, from the state of the country at the time, being then flooded, could not be ascertained; and that another river of no inconsiderable magnitude, fed by salt springs, was discovered by Captain Sturt on the 2d February last, about 100 miles to the westward of the Macquarie, running to the southward and westward.

By His Excellency's Command,

ALEXANDER M'LEAY.

Mount Harris, 4th March, 1829.

SIR,—I do myself the honor to acquaint you, for the information of His Excellency the Governor, that I returned to this eminence on Monday, the 23d ult. having been driven from the interior, in consequence of the extreme drought which prevails there.

I am to state, in reference to my former communication, that agreeably to what I then reported, I moved, on the 26th December last, lower down the plains of the Macquarie, but encountered a barrier of reeds, formed by the marshes of that river, through which we in vain endeavoured to force our way. I was in consequence obliged to make the nearest part of the river to my left, and to take such measures as the nature of my situation required. Here, for the first time, I set the boat afloat, deeming it

essential to trace the river, as I could not move upon its
banks, and wishing also to ascertain where it again issued
from the marshes, I requested Mr. Hume to proceed northerly, with a view to skirt them, and to descend westerly,
wherever he saw an open space. He was fortunate enough
to strike upon the channel about twelve miles north of our
position, but was obstructed in his further progress by another marsh, in consequence of which he returned to the
camp the next day; in the mean time, I had taken the
boat, and proceeded down the Macquarie, my way being
at first considerably obstructed by fallen timber: clearing
this obstacle, however, I got into a deeper channel, with
fine broad reaches, and a depth of from twelve to fifteen
feet water. I had a short time previously cleared all woods
and trees, and was now in the midst of reeds of great
height. After proceeding onwards for about eight miles
from the place whence I started, my course was suddenly
and unexpectedly checked; I saw reeds before me, and
expected I was about to turn an angle of the river, but I
found that I had got to the end of the channel, and that
the river itself had ceased to exist. Confounded at such
a termination to a stream, whose appearance justified the
expectation that it would have led me through the heart of
the marsh to join Mr. Hume, I commenced a most minute
examination of the place, and discovered two creeks, if
they deserve the name, branching, the one to the north-
west, and the other to the north-east; after tracing the
former a short distance, I reached its termination, and in
order to assure myself that such was the case, I walked
round the head of it by pushing through the reeds; it
being then too dark to continue where I was, I returned to

a place on the river, at which I had rested during a shower, and slept there. In the morning I again went to the spot to examine the north-eastern branch, when I was equally disappointed. I then examined the space between the two creeks, opposite to the main channel of the river, and where the bank receives the force of the current. Here I saw water in the reeds, but it was scarcely ankle deep, and was running off to the north-west quicker than the waters of the river, which had almost an imperceptible motion, I was therefore at once convinced that it was not permanent, but had lodged there in the night, during which much rain had fallen. I next pushed my way through the reeds into the marsh, and at length clearly perceived that the waters which were perfectly sweet, after running several courses, flowed off to the north, towards which point there was an apparent declination or dip. Finding it impossible to proceed further, I regained the boat, and thence returned to the camp, under a conviction that I had reached the very spot, at which Mr. Oxley lost the channel of the river in 1818.

The next day I moved to the place where Mr. Hume had struck upon the channel of the river, but was again doubtful in what direction to proceed.

The marsh, at the commencement of which we now found ourselves, being the third from Mount Foster, but the second great one, seemed to extend beyond us to the north for many miles, but varying in breadth. In the evening I went in the boat up the channel, and found it at first, deep and sullen, as that of the river above. It soon however, narrowed, and the weeds formed over its surface, so that I abandoned the boat and walked along a path up it. I had not gone far when the channel divided; two

smaller channels came, the one from the southern, and the
other from the western parts of the marsh into it. There
was an evident declination where they were, and it was at
their junction the river again rallied and formed. On my
return to the camp, Mr. Hume and I went down the river,
but found that about a mile it lost itself, and spread its
waters over the extensive marsh before it.

In this extremity, I knew not what movement to make,
as Mr. Hume had been checked in his progress north. I
therefore determined to ascertain the nature of the country
to the eastward and to the westward, that I might move
accordingly; I proposed to Mr. Hume, to take a week's
provisions, with two attendants, and go to the north-east,
in order again to turn the marsh, but with the expectation
that the angle formed by the junction of the Castlereagh
with the Macquarie would arrest its progress, as the last
was fast approaching the former.

I myself determined to cross the river, and to skirt the
marshes on the left, and in case they turned off to the north-
east, as they appeared to do, it was my intention to pursue
a N. W. course into the interior, to learn the nature of it.
With these views I left the camp on the 31st of December,
and did not return until the 5th of January. Having
found early in my journey, from the change of soil and
of timber, that I was leaving the neighbourhood of the
Macquarie, I followed a N. W. course, from a more north-
ernly one, and struck at once across the country, under an
impression that Mr. Hume would have made the river
again long before my return. I found, after travelling between twenty and thirty miles, the country began to rise;
and at the end of my journey, I made a hill of considerable

elevation, from the summit of which I had a view of other high lands; one to the S. W. being a very fine mountain. As I had not found any water excepting in two creeks, which I had left far behind me, and as I had got on a soil which appeared incapable of holding it, I made this this the termination of my journey, having exceeded 100 miles in distance from the camp, on my return to which I found Mr. Hume still absent. When he joined, he stated to me, that not making the Castlereagh as soon as he expected, he had bent down westerly for the Macquarie, and that he ended his journey at some gentle hills he had made; so that it appeared we must either have crossed each other's line of route, or that they were very near, and that want of length must alone have prevented them from crossing; but as such an assumption led to the conclusion that the Macquarie no longer existed, I determined to pursue a middle course round the swamps, to ascertain the point; as in case the river had ended, a westerly course was the one which my instructions directed me to pursue.

In the immediate neighbourhood of the marshes we were obliged to sink wells for water, and it was thus early that we began to feel the want of a regular supply.

Having made a creek about four miles from our position by cutting through the reeds where there was a narrow space, we pursued a westerly course over a plain, having every appearance of frequent inundation, and for four or five days held nearly the same direction; in the course of which we crossed both our tracks on the excursions we had made, which had intersected each other in a dense oak brush; thus renewing the few doubts, or rather the doubt

we had as to the fate of the Macquarie, whose course we
had been sent to trace.   Indeed, had I not felt convinced
that that river had ceased, I should not have moved westward without further examination, but we had passed
through a very narrow part of the marshes, and round the
greater part of them, and had not seen any hollow that
that could by any possible exaggeration be construed into
or mistaken for the channel of a river.

It appears, then, that the Macquarie, flowing as it does
for so many miles, through a bed, and not a declining country, and having little water in it, except in times of flood,
loses its impetus long ere it reaches the formidable barrier
that opposes its progress northwards; the soil in which
the reeds grow being a stiff clay.   Its waters consequently
spread, until a slight declivity giving them fresh impulse,
they form a channel again, but soon gaining a level, they
lose their force and their motion together, and spread not
only over the second great marsh, but over a vast extent
of the surrounding country, the breadth of ground thus
subject to inundation being more than twenty miles, and
its length considerably greater; around this space there is
a gentle rise which confines the waters, while small hollows in various directions lead them out of the marshes
over the adjacent plains, on which they eventually subside.
On my return from the interior, I examined those parts
round which I had not been, with particular attention,
partly in company with Mr. Hume, and this statement was
confirmed by what we saw.   Thus, at a distance of about
twenty-five miles from Mount Foster to the N.N.W. the
river Macquarie ceases to exist, in any shape as a river,
and at a distance of between fifty and sixty, the marshes

terminate, though the country subject to inundation from
the river is of a very considerable extent, as shewn by the
withered bullrushes, wet reeds, and shells, that are scattered over its surface.

Having executed the first part of the instructions with
which I had been honoured, I determined on pursuing a
west, or north-west course into the interior, to ascertain the
nature of it, in fulfilment of the second, but in doing this
I was obliged to follow creeks, and even on their banks
had to carry a supply of water, so uncertain was it that we
should meet with any at the termination of our day's
journey, and that what we did find would be fit to drink.
Our course led us over plains immediately bordering the
lower lands of the Macquarie, alternating with swamp oak,
acacia pendula, pine, box, eucalyptus, and many other
trees of minor growth, the soil being inclined to a red loam,
while the plains were generally covered with a black scrub,
though in some places they had good grass upon them.
We crossed two creeks before we made the hills Mr. Hume
had ascended, and which he called New Year's Range.
Around these hills the country appeared better — they are
gentle, picturesque elevations, and are for the most part,
covered with verdure, and have, I fancy, a whinstone base,
the rock of which they are composed being of various sub-
stances. I place New Year's Range in lat. 30° 21′,
long. 146° 3′ 30″. Our course next lying north-west along a
creek, led us to within twenty miles of the hill that had
terminated my excursion, and as I hoped that a more
leisurely survey of the country from its summit would open
something favourable to our view, I struck over for it,
though eventually obliged to return. From it Mr. Hume

and I rode to the S.W. mountain, a distance of about forty miles, without crossing a brook or a creek, our way leading through dense acacia brushes, and for the most part over a desert. We saw high lands from this mountain, which exceeds 1,300 feet in elevation, and is of sandstone formation, and thickly covered with stunted pine, in eight different points — the bearings of which are as follows: —

Oxley's Table Land, N. 40 E., distant 40 miles.

Kengall Hill, due E. very distant.

Conical Hill, S. 60 E.

Highland, S.E. distance 30 miles.

Highland, S. 30 E. distance 25 miles.

Long Range, S. 16 E. distance 60 miles.

Long Range, S. 72 W. distance 60 miles.

Distant Range, S. 25 W. supposed.

It was in vain, however, that we looked for water. The country to the north-west, was low and unbroken, and alternated with wood and plain.

The country from New Year's Range to the hill I had made, and which I called Oxley's Table Land, had been very fair, with good soil in many places, but with a total want of water, except in the creeks, wherein the supply was both bad and uncertain; on our second day's journey from the former, we came to the creek on which we were moving, where it had a coarse granite bottom. The country around it improved very much in appearance, and there was abundance of good grass on the surface of it, in spite of the drought. On the right of this creek, a large plain stretches parallel to it for many miles, varying in quality of soil. Near Oxley's Table Land, we passed over open forest, the prevailing timber of which was box. I have placed Oxley's Table Land in latitude 29° 57′ 30″, longitude 15° 43′ 30″.

Finding it impracticable to move westward from the hill, I again descended on the creek, whose general course was to the north-west, in which direction we at length struck upon a river whose appearance raised our most sanguine expectations. It flowed round an angle from the north-east to the north-west, and extended in longitude five reaches as far as we could see. At that place it was about sixty yards broad, with banks of from thirty to forty feet high, and it had numerous wild fowl and many pelicans on its bosom, and seemed to be full of fish, while the paths of the natives on both sides, like well-trodden roads, showed how numerous they were about it. On tasting its waters, however, we found them perfectly salt, and useless to us, and as our animals had been without water the night before, this circumstance distressed us much; our first day's journey led us past between sixty and seventy huts in one place, and on our second we fell in with a numerous tribe of natives, having previously seen some between two creeks before we made New-Year's Range. At some places the water proved less salt than at others; our animals drank of it sparingly: we found two small fresh-water holes, which served us as we passed. After tracing the river for a considerable distance, we came on brine springs in the bed of it, the banks having been encrusted with salt from the first; and as the difficulty of getting fresh water was so great, I here foresaw an end to our wanderings. And as I was resolved not involve my party in greater distress, I halted it, on overtaking the animals, and the next morning turned back to the nearest fresh-water, at a distance of eighteen miles from us. Unwilling, however, to give up our pursuit, Mr. Hume and I started with two men on horseback, to trace the river as far as we could, and to ascertain what course it took; in the hopes also that we should fall on some creek, or get a more certain supply of drinkable water. We went a distance to which the bullocks could not have been brought, and then got on a red sandy soil, which at once destroyed our hopes; and on tasting the river water we found it salter than ever, our supply being diminished to two pints. Our animals being weak and purged, and having proceeded at least forty miles from the camp, I thought it best to yield to circumstances, and to return, though I trust I shall be believed when I add, it was with extreme reluctance I did so; and had I followed the wishes of my party, I should still have continued onwards. Making a part of the river where we had slept, we staid to refresh, and in consequence of the heat of the weather were obliged to drink the water in it, which made us sick. While here, a tribe of blacks came to us and behaved remarkably well. At night we slept on a plain without water, and the next day we regained the camp, which had been visited by the natives during our absence.

We found the river held a south-west course, and appeared to be making for the central space between a high land, which I called Dunlop's Range, at Mr. Hume's request, and a lofty range to the westward. It still continued its important appearance, having gained in breadth and in the height of its banks, while there were hundreds of pelicans and wild-fowl on it. Flowing through a level country with such a channel, it may be presumed that this river ultimately assumes either a greater character, or that it adds considerably to the importance of some other stream. It had a clay bottom, generally speaking, in many places semi-indurated and fast forming into sandstone, while there was crystallized sulphate of lime running in veins through the soil which composed the bank.

This river differs from most in the colony, in having a belt of barren land of from a quarter of a mile to two miles in breadth in its immediate neighbourhood, and which is subject to overflow. This belt runs to the inland plains, where a small elevation checks the further progress of the flood. There is magnificent blue gum on both sides the river, but the right bank is evidently the most fertile, and I am mistaken greatly if there is not a beautiful country north of it.

Of the country over which we have passed, it is impossible for me to have formed a correct opinion under its present melancholy circumstances. It has borne the appearance of barrenness, where in even moderate rain, it might have shewn very differently, though no doubt we passed over much of both good and bad land; our animals on the whole, have thriven on the food they have had, which would argue favourably for the herbage. Generally speaking, I fear the timber is bad — the rough-gum may be used for knees, and such purposes, and we may have seen wood for the wheelwright and cabinet-maker, specimens of which I have procured, but none for general or household purposes.

The creeks we have traced are different in character from those in the settled districts, inasmuch as that, like the river, they have a belt of barren land near them and but little grass — they have all of them been numerously frequented by the natives, as appeared from the number of muscle-shells on their banks, but now having scarcely any water in them, the fish having either been taken, or are dead, and the tribes gone elsewhere for food, while the badness of the river water has introduced a cutaneous disease among the natives of that district, which is fast carrying them off. Our intercourse with these people was incessant from the time we first met them, and on all occasions they behaved remarkably well, nor could we have seen less than than two hundred and fifty of them.

Our return is to be attributable to the want of water alone, and it is impossible for me to describe the effects of the drought on animal as well as vegetable nature. The natives are wandering in the desert, and it is melancholy to reflect on the necessity which obliges them to drink the stinking and loathsome water they do—birds sit gasping in the trees and are quite thin — the wild dog prowls about in the day-time unable to avoid us, and is as lean as he can be in a living state, while minor vegetation is dead, and the very trees are drooping. I have noticed all these things in my Journal I shall have the honour of submitting through you, for the Governor's perusal and information, on my return. Finally, I fear our expedition will not pave the way to any ultimate benefit; although it has been the means by which two very doubtful questions, — the course of the Macquarie, and the nature of the interior, have been solved; for it is beyond doubt, that the interior for 250 miles beyond its former known limits to the W. N. W., so far from being a shoal sea, has been ascertained not only to have considerable elevations upon it, but is in itself a table land to all intents and purposes, and has scarcely water on its surface to support its inhabitants.

I beg you will inform His Excellency the Governor, that I have on all occasions received the most ready and valuable assistance from Mr. Hume. His intimate acquaintance with the manners and customs of the natives, enabled him to enter into intercourse with them, and chiefly contributed to the peaceable manner in which we have journeyed, while his previous experience put it in his power to be of real use to me. I cannot but say he has done an essential service to future travellers, and to the colony at large, by his conduct on all occasions since he has been with me; nor should I be doing him justice, if I did not avail myself of the first opportunity of laying my sentiments before the Governor, through you. I am happy to add that every individual of the party deserves my warmest approbation, and that they have, one and all, borne their distresses, trifling certainly, but still unusual, with cheerfulness, and that they have at all times been attentive to their duty, and obedient to their orders. The whole are in good health, and are eager again to start.

I have the honor to be,

Sir,

Your most obedient and most humble servant,

CHARLES STURT,

Capt. 39th Regt.

The Honorable The Colonial Secretary.

Mount Harris, 5th March, 1829.

SIR, — It having appeared to me, that after discovering such a river as the one I have described in my letter of yes-

terday, His Excellency the Governor would approve of
my endeavouring to regain it.   There being a probability
that it ultimately joins the Southern Waters, I thought of
turning my steps to the southward and westward; and with
a view to learn the nature of the country, I despatched Mr.
Hume in that direction on Saturday last.   He returned in
three days, after having gone above forty miles from the
river, and states, that he crossed two creeks, the one about
twenty-five miles, the other about thirty-two distance,
evidently the heads of the creeks we passed westward of
the marshes of the Macquarie.   He adds, that, to the second creek the land was excellent, but that on crossing it,
he got on a red soil, on which he travelled some miles further, until he saw a range of high land, bearing from him
S. W. by W., when, knowing from the nature of the country
around him, and from the experience of our late journey,
that he could not hope to find a regular supply of water in
advance, and that in the present dry state of the low lands,
a movement such as I had contemplated would be impracticable, he returned home.   I do myself the honour, therefore, to report to you, for His Excellency's information,
that I shall proceed on Saturday next in a N. E. direction
towards the Castlereagh, intending to trace that river down,
and afterwards to penetrate as far to the northward and
westward as possible; it being my wish to get into the
country north of the more distant river, where I have expectations that there is an extensive and valuable track of
country, but that in failure of the above, I shall examine
the low country behind our N. W. boundaries, if I can find
a sufficiency of water to enable me to do so.

I am to inform you that in this neighbourhood the

Macquarie has ceased to flow, and that it is now a chain of shallow ponds. The water is fast diminishing in it, and unless rain descends in a few weeks it will be perfectly dry.

I am also to report, that the natives attempted the camp with the supplies before my arrival at Mount Harris, but that on the soldier with the party firing a shot, after they had thrown a stone and other of the weapons, they fled. It was in consequence of their fires, which I saw at a distance of forty miles, and which they never make on so extensive a scale, except as signals when they want to collect, and are inclined to be mischievous, that I made forced marches up, and I am led to believe my arrival was very opportune. The natives have visited us since, and I do not think they will now attempt to molest either party when we separate.

I have the honour to be,

Sir,

Your most obedient and most humble servant,

CHARLES STURT,

Capt. 39th Regt.

The Hon. the Colonial Secretary.

END OF VOL. 1.

PRINTED BY STEWART AND CO., OLD BAILEY.

Lightning Source UK Ltd.
Milton Keynes UK
UKHW020628221222
414324UK00007B/667